A HEART
OF WISDOM

Marital Counseling with
Older and Elderly Couples

A HEART OF WISDOM

Marital Counseling with Older and Elderly Couples

Mary Ann Wolinsky, M.S.W.

BRUNNER/MAZEL, Publishers • New York

Library of Congress Cataloging-in-Publication Data

Wolinsky, Mary Ann.
    A heart of wisdom : marital counseling with older and elderly
couples / by Mary Ann Wolinsky.
        p.   cm.
    Includes bibliographical references.
    ISBN 0-87630-535-4
    1. Marriage counseling—United States.   2. Aged—Counseling of—
United States.   I. Title.
HQ10.5.U6W65   1990
362.82′86--dc20   90-35054
                                                       CIP

Published by
BRUNNER/MAZEL, INC.
19 Union Square West
New York, New York 10003

Designed by Thomas A. Bérubé
Manufactured in the United States of America

10 9 8 7 6 5 4 3 2 1

Contents

Introduction

The impact of longevity on personal life-style, family structure and function, and on society in general is enormous. Currently, people over 65 years old account for approximately 13 percent of the U.S. population, and it is estimated that their numbers will grow to 20 percent or more by the end of this century. Many changes associated with the greying of America have been positive, i.e., the growth of industries that meet the physical and social needs of an older population, larger family systems that can provide resources in coping with family problems in all generations, and the prospect for everyone of a longer, healthier, and more affluent life.

However, other changes have created problems for the aging individual, aging couples, and for their families. For instance, the social security and Medicare programs, which provide essential services for older Americans, are facing difficulties in meeting their financial obligations to the retired. Other concrete problems such as custodial care and transportation for the frail elderly are expensive and resistant to solutions. But, in the last analysis, the emotional problems associated with longevity appear to be the most difficult to contend with. Coping with long-term, chronic illness, the search for meaning in late life, and similar issues have brought many to the point of disillusionment with their golden years. Still, even with the serious and often sad events associated with growing old, most of us would not elect a shorter life span as a way to avoid the challenges of aging. Rather, we are a society that seeks solutions and cures. *A Heart of Wisdom* hopes to contribute ideas to that quest.

In order to discuss the subject of marriage in late life, it is necessary to point out the difficulties and problems of aging. However, it is one of the secondary goals of this book to emphasize the benefits to the individual, the family, and the society of having an older and more experienced segment of the population.

Attitudinal modifications about aging in the general population, including the aging and elderly themselves, are suggested that can ease the process of growing older and its impact on marriage in later life. Some of the issues that emerge in an aging population are discussed with emphasis on the changes, issues, and problems salient for older couples today. At the core of the book is a developmental marital counseling model that considers the developmental stage and task of the individual and the marital relationship. This model is specifically designed with the emotional and psychological assets and liabilities of an older population in mind.

It is essential that the reader be familiar with the attributes of the modern aging population. To that end, Chapter 1 presents the current facts and figures about older people that are forcing all of us, social scientists and family members alike, to reevaluate our ideas about the *process* of aging and what it is like to be "old." The elderly are no longer sick, poor, and mentally impaired, although such individuals are also members of the aging population. This chapter delineates the differences between being older, and the "frail elderly" who have so often served as our stereotype for what being old was all about. In fact, the average 65-year-old individual is vigorous and healthy and has a good chance of remaining so well into his or her 70s. He or she is likely to be well-educated, relatively affluent, and can afford vacations, hobbies, voluntary activities, an active social life and thus, is an economic and political force with which to be reckoned.

Chapter 2 discusses the modern family and the impact of current trends in family structure and function on the older generation. The physical distance that separates the generations of many families, along with the high rate of divorce, creates a great deal of isolation and loneliness for all members of today's family. This loneliness and isolation, coupled with prevailing values and expectations concerning the marital bond, has put great stress on marriages of older couples. They now have only each other with whom to face adversity and they too have come to expect the majority of their physical, social, and emotional needs to be met by one person—their spouse. In addition, a more permissive attitude toward divorce has opened this option for many older couples who would never have considered such a possibility even 20 years ago.

These present trends in the modern family, when coupled with longevity, have changed the character and issues in a marriage with mature partners. Marriage in later life has been termed in this book as "mature-stage marriage" and Chapter 3 discusses the issues and problems faced by the older, the aged, and the frail elderly couple. The issues are complex and difficult. They may be as mild as dealing with the changes in sexual function and personal appearance that go along with getting older, or they may be as devastating as the impact of chronic illness and disability, or of death and dying. Thus, the mature-stage marriage has very different developmental tasks than does the marital bond at earlier stages in life. Basically, these tasks concern validating the life of each individual partner, supporting the marital partners through retirement and the waning of physical powers, and maintaining the integrity of the marriage at the end of life itself.

As older couples face the personal and marital developmental tasks of late life, enormous psychological and social stresses are generated. Yet older people do not generally seek psychotherapy as a possible solution to problems. If they do seek help, they are often treated with the same expectations and treatment models developed for a much younger population. When they have not responded well within the standard psychotherapeutic frameworks, it has been concluded that they are not psychologically minded or no longer have the mental flexibility to benefit from psychotherapy. However, other age groups, or problem categories such as the sexually abused, have responded positively to specific therapies designed for them. The same is true for older people. Chapter 4 presents a treatment model designed for older and elderly couples. Their issues and concerns are not the same as a younger population, nor is their style of approaching problems. Older people appear to naturally return to the past as a way of validating their choices in life and making peace with themselves. The model utilizes this natural psychological process and the extensive personal and family history that has influenced the personality and life-style of an older person. Though the process is complicated and may be difficult, it can be immensely rewarding for the psychotherapist in terms of the opportunity to gain insights into recent history and in the modeling of the client of what growing older is all about.

Part II (beginning with Chapter 5) examines the developmental marital counseling model in depth beginning with the evaluation. Most marital counselors would agree that a good evaluation is essential for appropriate treatment planning and therefore is among the more important elements in the treatment process. The evaluation begins, as is customary, with a description of the problem that brings the couple into counseling. However, from this point on it becomes particularly complex because of the sheer numbers of people involved and the length of the history. It may include as many as four family generations, step-family ties, and a personal and family history of more than 70 years and a marital history as long as 50 or more years.

A crucial element of the evaluation is an assessment of the individual developmental stage and task of each partner and the developmental stage and tasks of the marriage. In the mature-stage marriage, unfortunately, the developmental stage and task of each partner and the marriage are not always in synchronization. When this situation occurs, the discrepancies may become a part of the marital problem. Chapter 6 explores developmental theory more in depth and its use in marital counseling with the older couple. Examples are given of how different developmental stage and task of the marital partners can adversely affect the marital bond—for instance, in the May-December marriage when one partner is considerably younger than the other. The older partner may be ready to retire just at a time when the younger partner is thinking much more seriously about deepening a professional commitment, or entering the work force, as many women are today after their children are grown and out of the house. Women, in general, are well behind their husbands in the process of developing a professional career. Retirement may present serious problems in terms of unmet expectations for companionship and understanding from both members of the couple.

A further important component of the developmental marital counseling model is the "marital life review." Robert Butler (1963) described a normal psychological process in older people he termed the life review. In this process, the individual reminisces about specific incidents in his or her life and about life in general. In remembering and rethinking these past events, the person has the opportunity to adjust his or her attitudes and values about particular events. Many older people make peace with themselves concerning traumatic events in their life and enhance and enrich their sense of integrity and self-worth in reviewing their achievements and triumphs. This self-actuating process can be evoked and focussed on the marriage, with the same beneficial effects.

No work with older individuals or couples is possible without paying attention to the resolution of loss and the grief process. Chapter 8 describes the role of grief therapy in marital counseling with older couples. Loss is inherent in the aging process. We are forced to adjust our expectations about self and career, older family members die, friends move away or die, and most important, we ourselves change. We begin to see the end of life. For all of these changes, people mourn. The process may be mild, or it may be severe, but it is there and it must be taken into account in the course of psychotherapy with the older couple.

The older couple often needs help of a concrete nature in restructuring roles and life-style. The last two chapters in Part II deal with the more action-oriented segment of the developmental marital counseling model. The psychotherapist now assumes an active, coaching and supportive role in helping the clients to seek new interests and developing new relationship styles. Educational, self-help, and social groups are utilized in aiding an individual or a couple in making necessary adjustments in the latter stages of the life cycle.

The final portion of the book deals with the special problems and issues in working with older couples and suggests new directions in problem solving and counseling techniques for use with an older population. First and foremost among the problems in working with older people is the reluctance of the therapist (Kastenbaum, 1964). Counter-transference issues such as unresolved issues with the psychotherapist's own parents, fear of aging, and death phobia, all contribute to the psychotherapist's reluctance to work with an aging population. Next in importance is the reluctance of the client. Older people have many prejudices, fears, and misconceptions about psychotherapy. This is in part due to lack of familiarity with psychotherapy and in part due to the realistic fears of giving up even more control of their lives than they are losing through the natural process of aging. Empathic and positive interpretations of these issues in ourselves as psychotherapists and of the client's resistances can open up new vistas in treatment with the elderly. There is the potential for a huge, untapped client population that needs help and can make use of help. The combination should provide an exciting climate for psychotherapeutic practice now and in the future.

PART I

History and Description of the Developmental Marital Counseling Model

1

Growing Older in America Today: New Facts, New Figures, A New Population

It is increasingly common to find older couples, veterans of long-term marriages, seeking psychotherapy for marital problems. This trend is due, in part, to the great numerical growth in the older population, to their increasing psychological awareness and to the complexity and severity of the problems and issues encountered during the latter stages of the aging process. Older couples are often a delight to work with. Even in the presence of major pathology, such as psychosis or mental impairment, their life experience pokes through from time to time, providing an extraordinary variety and depth to the psychotherapeutic interaction. As might be expected, older couples have wisdom, experience, and confidence in their own problem-solving ability. Years of coping with many and varied situations have taught them patience and complex methodology in the resolution of issues. Paradoxically, they also have an appreciation of simplicity and recognize the curative properties of time. In consequence, they will usually only seek psychotherapy when convinced that they have exhausted their own considerable coping skills.

The positive benefit to the therapeutic process is that a fair percentage arrive well prepared, with a great deal of preliminary work already accomplished. An older population brings many advantages to the therapeutic relationship. For them, introspection, reevaluation, and reminiscence are normally occurring psychological events.

They share readily a historical perspective that can give the therapist many insights into his or her personal background and the events which have shaped the present. Thus the psychotherapeutic relationship is rendered uniquely pleasurable and educational for the client and the therapist through the mutuality of the process. And, in the best tradition of psychoanalytic thought, since the sharing of thoughts and feelings produces a sense of well-being and resolution of conflict, the process is curative in itself.

TODAY'S OLDER GENERATION

We are accustomed to reading about an older generation that is poor, disadvantaged, frail, and in dire need of financial assistance and services, such as "Meals on Wheels." However, the large group of poverty-stricken elderly which once dominated the statistics is gradually disappearing. An examination of the demographic characteristics of the population over 65 provides valuable information and aids in the redefinition of today's older generations.

The 1986 figures compiled by the American Association of Retired Persons indicate that approximately 65% of families with head of household over the age of 65 had an income of $15,000 or more. Eighty percent of homeowners over 65 own their homes outright and many states offer property tax rebates for senior citizens. The cumulative effects of favorable laws, fewer dependent family members, and reduced financial obligations result in a higher percentage of discretionary income along with increased available income. Statistics support these conclusions and reflect that the poverty rate for persons over 65 is 12.6%, less than the 14.1% rate for the general population.

These older people have been called the "advantaged elderly" (Hellebrandt, 1980). It is important to note that this appellation does not refer solely, or even principally, to financial resources, but to a much more complicated and sophisticated mix of educational, financial, and social status. Fueled by the need for an ever more skilled and knowledgeable labor force, the educational level of the older population has been steadily increasing. Between 1970 and 1983, the median level of education in the population over 65 increased from 8.7 years to 11.0 years, and the percentage of high school graduates rose from 28% to 46%. Since median figures are used, we can deduce that a disproportionate amount of that level of education is located in the group termed "advantaged elderly." Furthermore, statistics indicate that if current fertility and immigration levels remain stable, the only age group to experience significant growth in the next century will be those over the age of 55. Presently, they represent 12% of the population, and by the year 2030, they are expected to represent 21.2% of the population. The percentage of poor elderly is gradually declining, and thus the advantaged elderly will represent 75% to 80% of the population over the age of 65 by the year 2000. But, we have already existing in our society, an enormous group of educated, relatively affluent, and highly sophisticated older and elderly individuals. Their numbers are growing and, if current trends in lengthening the life span continue, they will live to venerable ages.

PSYCHOTHERAPY WITH AN OLDER POPULATION

With all the potential and advantages older people have as productive members of society, little attention has been paid to their emotional and psychological needs. Their interests and concerns are poorly understood and their potential contributions to society are often ignored or bypassed (e.g., early retirement schemes). Their physical and financial needs are often viewed as threats (e.g., the somewhat spurious concerns about the costs of Medicare and the drain they present on public and private pension plans). They might be more accurately termed "the invisible advantaged elderly."

An important area of "invisibility" is in mental health services, and unfortunately the older generations themselves are partially responsible. In the short space of a generation or two, a major change has taken place in the attitude of the older population toward psychotherapy. People in their 60s appear to view psychotherapy from a different and more positive perspective than did their parents. Unfortunately, theoretical concepts regarding social and psychological services for senior citizens have been dominated by the characteristics and the needs of the highly visible and vulnerable proportion of the older population who are poor. So pervasive are these concepts that even the classic literature on psychotherapy with the elderly has been strongly impacted and until very recently, dictated drug therapy as the major treatment modality. Where psychotherapy was deemed appropriate, short-term crisis intervention and the provision of concrete services was the suggested treatment of choice (Goldfarb & Turner, 1953, Meerloo, 1961, and others). The gains made in psychotherapeutic techniques, such as family therapy and the advances in theoretical concepts, such as systems theory, ignored the older generations, except as historians and sources of information for the purpose of understanding the younger generations.

Classical theories on psychotherapy with an older population are based on the notions that older people are not psychologically sophisticated, are unable to afford psychotherapy, do not have sufficient remaining life span to justify the expenditure of time and effort for both the therapist and the client, and would not use psychotherapy in any case. While some initial reluctance to engage in the process of psychotherapy remains, these circumstances are no longer true for the majority of the elderly. But unfavorable attitudes toward psychotherapy with the elderly persist. They are strengthened by the tendency of older people to regard change with suspicion and to limit stimuli—factors which have led to the interpretation that older people are rigid in their thinking patterns and, thus, unable to change. Newer observations indicate that while older people are *slower* to adapt, they may actually be more adaptable than younger individuals.

Another part of the explanation may be that older people have traditionally made minimal use of psychotherapy and are underrepresented in all levels of social services. The customary explanation refers to the client's lack of familiarity and knowledge of available resources, or the psychotherapist's lack of interest or knowledge about this clientele. It is true that to many octogenarians alive today, psychotherapy was unknown and unheard of for the major part of their formative years, and that the accumulation of knowledge about the mental and emotional functioning of the older and elderly population is in its infancy. Probably the single greatest factor in the lack of knowledge about the elderly is simply that they did not exist in large enough numbers to be able to formulate a generalized body of knowledge concerning their lifestyle.

Unfortunately, the premise of mutual ignorance neglects many pivotal variables that effect the older person's willingness and/or ability to make use of the psychotherapeutic process.

VALUES AND ATTITUDES IN THE OLDER POPULATION

Conservative Values and Family-Oriented Expectations

Older people have the natural tendency to be conservative and reticent to discuss intimate issues outside the family circle. Older people have been taught to keep problems to themselves or within the family circle. They may consider the therapist and the psychotherapeutic process as intrusive rather than helpful. If they do share with the therapist, it is done with some guilt, as if having shared a forbidden secret. They expect that if any emotional help is needed, it will be supplied by a family member. They have not learned to accept the more formalized structure of help from social service agencies and mental health professionals.

Negative Attitudes Toward Psychotherapy

Their upbringing has taught many negative and prejudiced attitudes and ideas about emotional problems and mental illness. Not so long ago, the emotional and psychological determinants of human behavior were so little understood that psychosis was associated with the possession of supernatural powers and/or malingering. There was a widespread lack of sympathy for and fear of the insane. Many current negative attitudes toward psychotherapy have roots in these early beliefs, which persist in the elderly population. This is especially true among the very old: it is not uncommon for those in their 80s and 90s to consider the suggestion that they consult a psychotherapist about any topic, even the most benign, as an indication that they are thought to be "crazy." These suspicions are not entirely unrealistic and are rendered more threatening by some of the normal changes in mental functioning that accompany the aging process. When an older client population is strongly influenced by unfavorable values and prejudiced attitudes, they will most likely not make use of a standard psychotherapeutic approach and will respond much better to a group setting in which the principal agenda is not directly referred to as psychotherapy, such as a *reminiscence group*.

Socially Acceptable Feelings and Behavior

Four thousand years ago, the Greeks began observing and chronicling the complexities in human relationships, with remarkable astuteness. Many of their observations became underpinnings in modern psychoanalytic thought. They noted the association between intense emotions and potentially destructive behavior and sought to use the intellect to modify impulse and glorify reason. A legacy of suspicion and negative interpretation about the emotions was left in Western, Judeo-Christian cultures. Intense feelings often became confused with the control of impulsive behavior because of the close association. It has been thought that not only should feelings be controlled, but also they could be controlled by the imposition of reason and order through the medium of the intellect, the expectation being that as soon as the "feelings" are brought under control, behavior will follow suit.

It was only some 100 years ago that Freud, and a few early pioneers, began to explore the continent of the emotions and feelings and defined them as useful, positive, and integral components of the human organism. The roles played by the powerful positive and negative emotions that shape human behavior have been recognized, and since that time, we have been engaged in an ongoing process of describing the causes and functions of human emotions. Older people tend to favor the more traditional values about what, when and how the expression of strong emotions is acceptable. They may be suspicious of the process of exploration of feelings inherent in psychotherapy and are much more likely to be interested in learning to control feelings rather than understanding them.

VARIABLES IN SOCIETY

Social Prejudice Concerning Aging and the Aged

In America, we play the numbers game. Some of the more significant numbers have become a part of our culture. For instance, "You can't trust anybody over 30" has become enshrined as the "generation gap." If you are over 40, you have lost your sex appeal. (There are interesting developments as movie stars age and refuse to give up their sex symbol status roles). At 50, it's all downhill and at 65, *you are old.*

There are many pejorative myths associated with growing older: the elderly are considered to be nonproductive, sick, mentally incompetent, a drain on their families and on society, asexual or perverted, humorless, mean, impatient, uninterested and uninteresting, lacking in understanding of young people, and self-centered. Our societal values support a negative attitude toward aging. We appreciate achievement, success, activity, work, efficiency, practicality, progress, external conformity, science, and rationality.

Unfortunately, every one of these values is antithetical to the aging process and to old people. The end result is that the elderly, especially the frail elderly, have become strangers in a society that they have participated in making, but in which they are minimally involved and no longer belong.

These myths and attitudes are associated with our deepest fears about our own aging process and our feelings about death. They are generally referred to as *ageism*. Ageism is the single most powerful determining factor affecting the provision and use of social services of all categories. It cuts across age barriers so that not only do younger people have a negative stereotype of older people, but the elderly themselves, through intolerance and ignorance of the aging process when younger, have first created and then incorporated these attitudes. The resulting loss in self-esteem enormously complicates the emotional work which older persons need to accomplish if they are to maintain a meaningful, positive life-style in the last years of life.

How Did "Old" Get to Be "Useless"?

The elderly were not always viewed in such an unfavorable light. In colonial times, age—not youth—was exalted. The old were believed to be in favor with God. Their long lives indicated that they would go to heaven and, concomitantly, the Bible was interpreted to mean that the good person would be rewarded with long life. Even the fashions, especially for men, seemed to emulate age. Clothing made the shoulders appear narrow and the waist and hip broad. The spine appeared somewhat bent. Both sexes wore powdered, white wigs (Barrow & Smith, 1979).

Respect for the elderly was rooted not only in religious and political ideology, but also in legal and financial reality. The elderly owned and controlled the land, the major source of livelihood. During this period of favor, they were a very select group in other ways as well, accounting for less than 3% of the population. On the negative side, along with the respect and favor with which they were viewed, came responsibility. Older people, no matter what their circumstances or state of health, were expected to be role models of service and virtue in the community. Social pressure to live up to ideal standards of conduct was great. This period of gerontophilia lasted from about 1600 to approximately the early 1800s. Toward the end of the 1700s, an era of deep political, economic, and social changes began the modification in attitude toward the elderly. The growth of industrialization loosened the reins of the older population on the means of livelihood, and as America increasingly moved away from a traditional agricultural society, the old lost power and favor. They became a burden in an industrial society where, when they lost the ability to work, they lost the ability to care for themselves financially. This was an era of growing gerontophobia, as Americans increasingly glorified youth instead of age, and the elderly often became victims of prevailing attitudes and social arrangements (Barrow & Smith, 1979).

The aged population grew rapidly during the late 1800s and the early 1900s. Retirement became common, although many old people had no source of income. As medical and technological advances grew and ensured that more and more older people were evident in society, their problems finally became obvious and significant enough to trigger another great attitudinal change toward the elderly. Old age began to be perceived as a social problem, and an elaborate system of social welfare was created to deal with it. This is essentially the social and political situation that has existed until very recently. Another period of transition is underway. For the first time, the older people exist in large enough numbers to make their power felt not only through the control of economic resources, but through sheer numbers as well. The pros and cons of this phenomenon are growing more evident all the time.

PSYCHODYNAMIC ISSUES IN THE AGING PROCESS

At the core of a sense of identity and self-worth are dependency issues and the imminence of death. Thus, the basic psychodynamic issues salient for older adults concern the maintenance of self-worth and physical integrity. Daily activities which reflect individuals' interests and engage their emotions (i.e., positive social and relational) and a sense of basic security (i.e., the knowledge that one has the necessary shelter, clothing, food, and medical care to maintain life) are the stuff of which a meaningful life-style is constructed for older adults.

However, being "old" is regarded so negatively that dealing with normal aging processes and issues has become problematic for us. At no other stage of life do we experience such definitive cutoffs and far-reaching role changes. A negative attitude from society, based on prejudice, fear, and an antithetical value system, obviously chips away at an older person's personal integrity and sense of worth, weakening coping mechanisms at a critical time. When these negative attitudes have been incorporated extensively by an aging individual, psychological defenses may be easily overwhelmed and severe depression and emotional illness can result. This process contributes considerably to the overrepresentation of the elderly among the patients on hospital psychiatric wards.

It is not surprising that denial of the aging process has become institutionalized into social mores. Not only are major personal investments of emotional and physical effort engaged in holding off the "markers" of age and death, but a fair proportion of the social and financial resources of the nation are involved as well.

We deny our aging process in a variety of ways (e.g., plastic surgery, dying our hair, lying and joking about our ages). It is considered impolite to ask people how old they are. In fact, it is against the law to ask prospective employees how old they are, so entrenched has the negative attitude toward older people become in recent years. How and when we get to be old is a major issue in our society and those at the beginning of the latter stages of the life cycle may be fearful, anxious, and involved in denying the process rather than enjoying what it has to offer.

THE DEVELOPMENTAL ISSUES OF AGING

Socially defined time is interwoven with the biological and chronological measurements of time. Each society is age graded and has a system of social expectations regarding age-appropriate behavior. The individual passes through a regulated social cycle from birth to death as inexorably as he passes through a biological cycle. And for the foreseeable future, human beings will grow and develop to biological, psychological, and social maturity in the first third of the life span, will continue to change psychologically and socially in the second and third parts of the life span, and finally, will biologically decline and die. Expectations regarding age-appropriate behavior form an elaborate and pervasive system of norms governing behavior and provide one of the basic guidelines to social interaction. For instance, these norms determine the ways in which different age groups relate to each other, and operate as a system of checks and balances on behavior. Each age group has recognized rights, duties, and responsibilities and the internalization of age norms and age group identification are important dimensions of the social and cultural context in which the course of the individual life span is viewed (Neugarten & Datan, 1973). There is a prescriptive timetable for the ordering of life events, probably already ancient when so beautifully described by the Old Testament in Ecclesiastes 3: "For everything there is a season, a time to live, a time to die. . . ." The timing of life events, and the reactions and adaptations of individuals to life events that occur out of schedule, provide powerful clues to the adult personality.

People are aware not only of the biological, chronological, and social clocks that operate in the various areas of their lives, but also of their own timing and readily describe themselves as early, late, or on time in relation to major life events. Furthermore, it may be that the social clock can have far-reaching impact on biological longevity. One study showed that the upper middle class did not consider themselves old until age 70, but working-class individuals considered themselves old at 60. Since how we view ourselves has impact on behavior, which in turn, affects physical and psychological health, a sense of well-being, and the quality of life, it is not difficult to infer an impact on longevity.

The other major issue that concerns older people is death and dying. Enhanced technology and changing family structure have affected the end of the life cycle profoundly. Life can now be prolonged for lengthy periods of time. Unfortunately, for many, this has meant a lengthy period of dependency and pain. Older people often express a fear of being dependent and a burden to their families. Living wills and instructions to family members regarding preferences concerning treatments and lifesaving measures are some of the strategems and decisions that concern people today. Euthanasia has become a major legal issue as people are confronted with the horrors of degenerative diseases such as cancer and Alzheimer's Disease. Issues of "the right to die" and "what is death?" are likely to remain with us. They force us, as a society, to deal with death differently. We may yet be faced with making the choice of a day and hour for our death.

If the primary developmental issue in the late aging process is the validation of life in the face of eventual death, then the primary developmental issue in the early aging process is life without work. With the loss of the "meaningful activity" of work that is inherent in retirement, a major task in the early latter stages of the life cycle is to find a suitable substitute for the workplace. This problem used to be confined mainly to males, but as more and more women enter the work force, they will face the same issues. Unfortunately, the concept of retirement enjoyed a very short vogue that was tied to the economic prosperity of the 1960s and 1970s. People looked forward to the opportunity to rest, travel, and to learn new skills and hobbies. The idea of leisure time to do nothing was valued.

Today, retiring individuals may just as likely regard retirement as being "put out to pasture"—a reflection of the feelings of uselessness and isolation engendered by ageism. This attitude is an outgrowth of the insecurity in the workplace and the resultant emphasis on "productivity."

FAMILY DEVELOPMENTAL ISSUES

The Mature-Stage Marriage

It is the family—the relationships within a family, both past and present—that contribute most to an older person's sense of self-worth and accomplishment. Therefore, in a successful aging process, the marital relationship, followed by the extended family relationships, is pivotal in constructing a meaningful life-style for older and elderly persons.

Once adult children have established their own families, there is a period of time that may last for as long as 30 or 40 years (depending on the age of childbearing and the health of the older generation parent) when the older generations of the family consist of the marital dyad. During this period, the adult child/adult parent roles remain more or less stable. The relationship is one of equals and the familial relationship style sets the boundaries to the interactions between the generations. Emotional ties are strong, but the central emotional commitment is to the marital relationship rather than the parent/child bond.

While it lasts, the marital tie is the basic family relationship which offers emotional and physical companionship in later life and is one of the few sources of physical closeness available to the elderly. As we age, one of the greatest losses we experience is the opportunity for physical touching and sexual expression with other human beings. As the marital partners begin to experience the physical disabilities associated with growing older, sexual expression assumes a secondary role and the opportunity for physical touching and nurturance become primary. The physical needs of the couple tend to absorb ever greater amounts of physical and emotional energy as the couple attempts to compensate for functional deficits. With isolation from other social and relational interaction, mutual dependency, be it positive or negative in nature, increases until the marital tie is dissolved by death (or in rare cases at this stage, by divorce).

The Intergenerational Family System

With increasing age, the extended family unit, consisting of three, four, and sometimes even five generations, begins to assume an increasingly central role in the psychodynamic life of the elderly individual.

The notion of "invisible loyalty" explored by Boszormenyi-Nagy and Spark in their book, *Invisible Loyalties* (1973) is useful in conceptualizing the relationship between adult parents and adult children. Children feel obligated and responsible to their parents, and parents know that ultimately they have a right to expect children to provide for them when they themselves are no longer able. These feelings are very strong, whether they are overt and expressed or unconscious and silent. As Boszormenyi-Nagy (1973) expressed it, "My father will always remain my father. . . . he and I are two consecutive links in a genetic chain with a life span of millions of years. My existence is unthinkable without his . . . he was obligated to me, his son, and, subsequently, I have become existentially indebted to him" (p. 3).

As the older generation ages and begins to lose ability to function, the adult parent and adult child relationship begins to assume greater importance; and emotionally, the relationship becomes charged once again. Unresolved issues recycle now through the relationship between the generations; and, again, these parent-child issues may play out in the marital relationship of both generations. This occurs as a result of the generational task shift in the caregiving functions from the older generation to the adult children. This gradual role change, involving the parent's ability to express dependence and the adult child's ability to accept that dependence, is called *filial maturity* (Blenkner, 1965). It represents a loss for both the older generation and the adult child. If not accomplished empathically and supportively, it may synergistically and negatively affect the physical and mental losses that are taking place in the older generation and may hasten the decline in function.

CONCLUSIONS

Due to advances in medicine, public health, nutrition, and life-style, the modern older generation is a population with a wide range in chronological age and functional capacity. The latter stages of the life cycle now account for almost half of the entire life span. At the beginning of this century, life expectancy was 47 years. Today, a 47-year-old person is only in the early stages of the last half of his or her life span. However, individuals of this age have begun to experience the physical, mental, and emotional changes that herald the end of life in themselves personally, and in the members of their family and friends. The average person of 65, while experiencing some physical and medical problems, is probably physically active and personally attractive. The chronological age at which people begin to suffer serious debility as a function of the aging process has now moved to about 75. In acknowledgment of this phenomenon, the distinction is now made between the "young old" (ages 65 to 75) and the "old old" (past age 75).

Thus, a large proportion of the older generation are relatively young in age and are at the height of their physical and mental productive capacities, while others are very aged and near death. It is helpful to think of members of the older generations on a continuum, with individuals who are intact physically and mentally on one end, the frail elderly on the other end, and the rest at all stages of physical and mental competence in between. They are defined as older not only, or even mainly, due to chronological age, but because of the life cycle events which are a part of their daily activities and concerns. Furthermore, it is these life cycle events and tasks that determine the developmental stage of the individual or couple. Thus, the "older couples" referred to in this book range in age from the mid-40s to the 80s, 90s, or even older. Naturally, their functional capacities and the concerns that motivate them to seek psychotherapy will vary greatly.

As we seek to understand the events and tasks inherent in the latter stages of the life cycle, and why some people age better than others, we are beginning to see clues that indicate that a complicated interplay of physiological, psychological, social, and environmental factors probably determine how we grow and thrive. A definite shift is taking place, away from the chronological and disease models, in our view of the aging process. Guides to successful aging are now being sought, not only in the usual areas of genetic history and physical fitness, but in ambiguous areas such as the degree of loneliness people experience and the sense of control that they feel over their lives. The issues of control, autonomy, and dependency are at the core of work with persons in the latter years of the life cycle. These issues play out in the marriage and in society, and at this stage of life they return with renewed vigor to the extended family system as well. Within this context, the role of marriage and the family has been shown to be crucial to both quality and longevity in life.

2

Changes in Modern Family Life-style: Implications and Trends in the Older Population

The family is the most ubiquitous, enduring, and close-knit locus of direct relationships for the individual. It is bound together by the intense and long-lasting ties of past experiences, social roles, mutual support, and expectations. Each family is a milieu consisting of family myths and scripts, values, traditions, membership and personality; that is, differences in feeling, thinking, styles of interaction and coping mechanisms used to deal with problems, trauma and stress. It has substantial resources in the form of physical and emotional health, social ties (i.e., the number of family members, kin, friends and social group memberships), and financial and economic assets.

Yet, for all its strengths and endurance, family stability, in terms of structure, function, and role, cannot be taken for granted. Patterns in American family life are changing rapidly, and while the locus of change often occurs in the younger generations, the impact is reflected in the life-style of older and elderly Americans. Traditional patterns, roles, and support structures in the aging generation of the family are especially affected, with positive and negative results.

CHANGES IN FAMILY STRUCTURE AND FUNCTION

The dominant form of family life in America at the turn of the century was the extended family. It was characterized by a large number of blood-related individuals, with their spouses and children, living in a relatively small geographical area and accepting leadership from a patriarchal family member. Decisions were made by the family leadership for its individual members and were based on potential benefit to the family, rather than the individual. Social status and profession were often determined by family membership and the extended family unit was solely responsible for all dependent family members, young or old (Blau, 1973). Children were an economic asset, especially in rural areas, and since effective birth control was not available and as many as half of children died in infancy, large families were the rule in order to ensure the continuation of the family (and the species) and to help with family chores, especially (Stein & Cloward, 1958). In the more affluent families, male members of the household carried the responsibility for financial and economic support. Women of lower economic status, and those who lived on farms, worked, but their contribution to family financial survival received little recognition. The opposite was often true: the working woman was often a symbol of the family's failure to succeed economically and socially.

The advent of the technological revolution accelerated the changes in the structure and function of the family begun by industrialization. Universal education spread rapidly and centered in schools in order to meet the need for technological knowledge and the family lost the function of educating new members into a profession. Children began to require a lengthy period of dependence during the preparation for a trade or profession and they became a long-term responsibility of the family. The trend of lengthening dependency on the family of origin still persists and is one of the major factors accounting for smaller families today.

Families began to break up into component parts in order to take advantage of newly created economic opportunities (Ackerman, 1958). Geographic mobility became common and expectable, so that the communities we live in now are as much cultural as they are geographic. This condition reduces the sense of uprootedness that often accompanies a change of location, but may add to the isolation between the subgroups and generations of a family. The resultant family structure, called the intact nuclear family, consists of the biological father, the biological mother, and usually two or three children. The decade of the 1950s was the zenith of this family form and today it is often still regarded as the ideal form of family life. It provides personal stability with the least amount of individual responsibility to the family unit and promotes significant individual independence while maximizing the potential for financial and professional achievement and success of the individual members and the family unit.

However, this family form has not been durable and only 30 years later accounts for less than half of existing families. Along with one of the highest marriage rates, America has one of the highest divorce rates. The remarried family now accounts for a significant percentage of family units, and there are indications that it may even replace the intact nuclear family (Visher & Visher, 1979). The control of pregnancy (begun in the 1950s) dramatically restructured our family life and our society, in terms of sexual mores, relationship styles, gender roles, and employment patterns. As values changed, the proscriptions of society were loosened. Now, more than at any other time in history, young people are deciding not to get married at all (Grunebaum & Christ, 1976). Among these single people is a large group of individuals who are choosing alternate life-styles. Most of these individuals will form long-term relationships which share most of the characteristic structural traits, roles, and functions of a family, even though society has failed to recognize these relationships, either socially or legally. Therefore, these individuals are treated as singles in the family and in the community. Whether singles live alone or in a nonformalized union, they nonetheless participate in a family structure (Carter & McGoldrick, 1980).

Marriage once defined maturity within the family and in society. This is no longer the case, as younger family members often marry before they have completed the preparation necessary for economic independence. Conversely, large numbers of singles are delaying marriage and childbearing, probably due to young women choosing to go on for a higher education. Many married couples are electing not to have children at all. First marriages are entered into at a later age, and the intervals between marriage and divorce and divorce and remarriage are shortening.

A more recent change, but one with far-reaching implications, is the emergence of the family in which both caregivers work. Some figures indicate that more than half of married women are in the work force. The immediate impact on the modern family has been the inclusion into the family structure of peer groups, teachers, and other ancillary groups to provide intimacy, emotional support, help, companionship, and role models for dependent family members in the absence of a full-time family caregiver. This expanded structure has been referred to as the "everyday family" (Visher & Visher, 1979).

While the quantity of tasks and functions performed by the family has declined steadily, the prospect of achieving those remaining goals has grown much more complex and difficult. Some current roles and functions that the family maintains are:

- assuring the continuation of the species
- socializing the next generation
- providing a mutual emotional support system
- acquiring and distributing goods and services within the family to ensure survival of all the generations in the family
- preparing for retirement (a relatively new role)
- providing or arranging for the physical care of frail, elderly family members
- preparing for death

In order to accomplish these tasks, the modern family operates as a combination of loosely allied subgroups that exist within an extended social boundary system—hereafter referred to as the family network system (see Figure 1).

THE FAMILY NETWORK SYSTEM

Modern family life-style bears remarkable resemblance to a kinship model of family life, with parents (the caregiving generation) relying increasingly on the temporary induction of community and informal social support systems into the family to fulfill some traditional family functions, such as care for dependent family members. Within this boundary, interpersonal and intergenerational alliances can shift according to need. Collateral social and institutional groups, such as schools and peer groups, are periodically incorporated into the family system, according to the needs and/or involvement of individual family members. There is a graded organization of family ties and loyalties. The closest ties are between the nuclear family subgroup and its biological relatives. These ties gradually loosen with distance in biological and group relationship. An example is the school tie, which is extremely strong during the period of association. However, this is a transitory group membership and while memories and links may continue, basic ties fade away.

The boundaries and the functions of the family have become so fluid and intermixed with other institutions in society that, at times, appropriate expectations are still unclear and require negoti-

FAMILY NETWORK SYSTEM

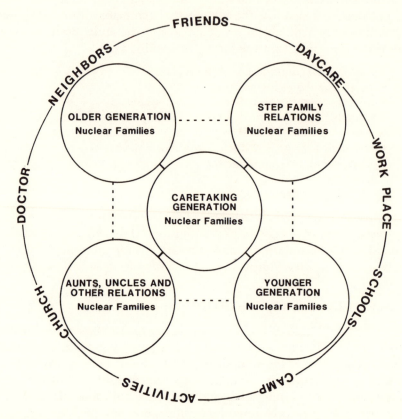

Figure 1

ation. This is especially valid in intergenerational relations and expectations concerning older generations. It is ironic that the quest
for personal freedom that enabled the pursuit of individual interests and goals has resulted in a powerful bond with social and economic institutions. For some, the "tyranny" of the social institution
has replaced the "tyranny" of the family. However, it may be more
comfortable to conform to the rules and regulations of the more distant social institutional group than to the closer ties of the extended
family.

Because of rapidly changing roles and structure, the modern
nuclear family has been viewed as isolated and at risk. There is concern that the family is disintegrating rather than only changing.

There are recent indications that the rapid rate of change in the family may now be stabilizing as a new age of restraint is ushered is, fueled by economic downturn, the emergence of serious sexually transmitted diseases, the difficulties and loneliness of being a single parent, and the complexities of parenting from two separate households.

It appears that the dominant form of the American family will be the remarried family, with both members of the couple employed, and children belonging to two or more family systems. Large minority groups will consist of single-parent families and singles, i.e., those who have never married, or who are widowed or divorced and have never remarried and therefore live alone, but who will nonetheless participate in a family network system (Carter & McGoldrick, 1980).

Implications for the Generations of the Family

In order to comprehend how these changes and shifts are felt by the older members of the family, it is necessary to understand the impact on the younger generations. To begin with, today's remarried family is culturally disadvantaged (Visher & Visher, 1979). It is difficult for society to shift values quickly and new family forms are emerging in a climate where old family concepts linger. Divorce is still considered a failure and bears some stigma whereas the intact nuclear family is often held up as the desirable family form, even though it is no longer dominant.

In addition to the issues of self-worth that are raised in divorce and remarriage, the legal codes and laws favor the biological family. These legal realities can be detrimental to stepfamily functioning in two ways. First, they increase the confusion of family roles for the new family. The new stepparent has no legal status in relation to stepchildren, which can increase the difficulties in accepting role and function for both the stepparent and the child. Second, children of divorced families are often suffering severe emotional and financial trauma directly associated with the failure of the law to protect their rights through the enforcement of child support payments and the protection of visitation and custody rights (Visher & Visher, 1979). Kidnapping has become a major problem in this country, as parents take the law into their own hands and are not prevented from doing so.

Structurally, the stepfamily has many elements that are quite different from the intact nuclear family and that create complex and difficult situations. Traditionally, the family has always been a boundaried entity within the social structure of society. Stepfamily boundaries must be much more permeable to allow for multiple entries and exits from the family structure and to allow for the presence of the other natural parent with power, outside the stepfamily boundary. Disputes over holidays, special events, illness, and so on, are common. Furthermore, there is a proliferation of persons with or without power, but with claims to family membership, which has led to an increasing sense of dislocation, alienation, and confusion for marital partners as to their appropriate roles and functions. Because of the permeable boundaries in stepfamilies, even when the parental partners have considerable control, individual members need flexibility and a tolerance for ambiguity.

This ambiguity includes the ghosts of all the former relationships for the different family members. Each family member has experienced the rupture of some family bond and the emotional leftovers from these former relationships can complicate the building process for the new family due to fear of failure, incongruent traditions, and invalid or irrelevant rules and regulations. The expression of anger and disagreements may become difficult if they are viewed as signals for dissolution, and the resolution of normal stresses and strains may become complicated (Visher & Visher, 1979). With the basic structure and function of the family thus under attack, the peripheral members of the family (i.e., the elderly living in separate households), may well receive less than their fair share of family care and attention.

The changes in the caregiving generation (i.e., the marital couple of childbearing age or who have already given birth to children) of the modern family have profound effects for the older generations in the family, not only in terms of the interaction between the generations, but in terms of internal structure, function, and role within the older generation.

A foremost issue for all of the generations is the confusion about which individuals belong "in the family" (Wolinsky, 1986). The older couple today cannot expect their adult children to marry only once and produce grandchildren with one person. Today, they can expect to see their child marry twice, and possibly three or four times and their grandchildren may be parented by two or more "other" parents. Unfortunately, the prejudices and values of the older generation can operate to create difficulties. Older generations have been socialized to view divorce negatively and to assume that the stepparent will not be as good as the biological parent. The remarriage may be viewed from that negative framework. In addition, grandparents often step in after a divorce to take care of grandchildren and relate to the parent—their child—as they did before the parent's marriage. They may feel displaced and become hostile toward the new spouse.

In the same vein, but posing a different dilemma for the older generation, is the issue of the spouses of the biological child, especially if that spouse has custody of the grandchildren. In order to maintain access to grandchildren, the older generation may have a greater need to maintain relationships with their children's ex-spouses than their children do. This is a further complication in family relationships.

Then there is the issue of grandparenting stepgrandchildren. This relationship may be very difficult to build, since grandparents are quite removed from the stepchild in the family and often do not have much of an opportunity to get to know this child. Special circumstances often need to be structured if a meaningful stepgrandparenting relationship is to occur. Unfortunately, all too often, the lack of an existing relationship between intergenerational members of the stepfamily is ignored and feelings get hurt because relationships with biological grandchildren differ from those with stepgrandchildren. Grandparents are often asked by their children to support the new marriage by forging bonds with children with whom they are unfamiliar, and who may later be lost to them through divorce. It is a very difficult situation which can create or add to emotional distance between the biological generations of a family.

Perhaps the gravest concern for the older generation has to do with their legal rights in this stepfamily structure. At the present time, in most states, grandparents have no legal rights regarding biological grandchildren or stepgrandchildren, but especially in the latter case. Visitation privileges may be denied to grandparents, and often their only recourse is to sue for custody of the grandchildren. Where stepgrandchildren are concerned, even this recourse is unavailable. Lately, there has been some response to this problem. For instance, recently the Texas Family Code was amended to allow grandparents to sue for rights of access to their grandchildren, without having to sue for custody.

The loss of grandchildren to the older generation is extremely serious. The elderly members of today's families are already concerned about the availability of a family caregiver if they become frail. But even greater than the loss of potential caregivers is the loss of people to love and be loved by. As we grow older, people we love, and who have loved us, die, and our memberships in social systems begin to diminish (Neugarten, 1964). In extreme old age, the family may be the only social system in which membership is still maintained. As families have become smaller, any loss of family members becomes very serious, and may even be irreplaceable. Sheer numbers are a potential family strength and, certainly for the aged, can provide variety in human relationships and warmth in their final days.

Perhaps the most important aspect of maintaining a relationship with grandchildren involves the role of family continuity in resolving the dilemma of personal death. A strong and warm relationship with grandchildren provides older people with a sense of continuity of a piece of themselves, of the family, and symbolizes an investment in the future that they will not be there to see. Such conditions help them to accept the inevitability of death.

Although exits and entries to the family network system are rapid and highly complex, and the criteria for family membership often cause difficulty for the older generations of the family, this new family configuration has rich sources of potential strengths for its older generations. Its membership is numerous and experienced in relationships and offers the opportunity for increased variety in interpersonal contacts with the extended stepfamily structures (Visher & Visher, 1979). Relationships are often forged with spouses of children and stepgrandchildren that are lifelong and offer the older generation opportunities to do better the second time around with collateral family relationships. Also, older family members who need help have a larger pool of individuals who might be called on to participate in caregiving, relieving the nuclear caregiving generation of the family network system of the total responsibility for meeting the normal and expectable dependency needs of their older relatives. And, the older generations have less necessity to compromise independent decision making or life-style in order to receive custodial care.

CHANGES IN THE STRUCTURE AND FUNCTION OF OLDER FAMILIES

Remarriage

The older generation of the family is also contributing new members to the family system and adding to the complexities and ambiguities of the entire system. As physical health improves and longevity increases, there is a growing tendency to remarry after the death of a spouse. This trend is accelerated slightly by a small but measurable increase in the divorce rate of older couples (Glick & Kessler, 1980). Older men almost always remarry, whereas older women may not. This is a function of two variables: lack of suitable partners, especially in later years when women outnumber men so greatly; and the cultural value that assigns women to the caregiver role. Many older women, having tasted independence, do not want to lose it. Then, too, there is the unwillingness to risk a new object loss. Many older women express the fear that they will remarry only to find themselves a caregiver and nurse until their spouse dies and they are alone once again. This is, of course, a realistic fear.

The older couple faces many significant barriers to success from adult children, differences in life-style and habits, and expectations shaped in other relationships. Froma Walsh (Carter & McGoldrick, 1980) notes that a critical variable in the success of late life remarriage is the approval of adult children and the subsequent relationship established within the enlarged, extended family. While it is not necessary for the new spouse to parent adult children, the inclusion of the adult children of both spouses into the extended family system and the sensitive understanding of the reciprocal emotional, financial, and physical support systems that exist between parents and their adult children are essential for the development of a positive marital relationship. Other difficulties may arise from the adult children if the remarriage is viewed as disloyalty to the deceased parent or if there is strife over property and inheritance. Financial issues are common enough that the prenuptial agreement is often used before remarriage in the latter stages of the life cycle. If the prenuptial agreement is not possible, other arrangements are often concluded prior to the marriage.

Another major problem in remarriage of older people is role definition. The roles of husband and wife are often ill defined and may be contaminated by the expectations generated in the previous marriage and the expectations of the adult children. Often, with older couples, one member of the couple will move into the partner's neighborhood, physically and emotionally, which may increase the difficulties of role redefinition.

Difference in life-style is the difficulty individuals have in tolerating and accepting the feelings, needs, opinions, and ways of doing things that are different from their own. In remarriage, especially for the older couple, this difficulty is a major barrier to interpersonal harmony. The differences that need to be worked out are magnified considerably by the complexity of the family structure and the marital and parental patterns of each member of the couple that have developed and solidified before the present relationship. Disability and dependency often activate anxiety about death and dying in the caregiver and impact negatively on the older marital couple and on the family network system. The following case example illustrates how the interaction of aging issues, role definition problems in a second marriage, and inappropriate expectations of and from adult children and stepchildren may seriously jeopardize the marital bond in late life.

Case Example

Presenting Problem. Mr. and Mrs. D were an elderly couple, married for a second time for the past three years. They were referred for counseling by one of Mrs. D's two children, both of whom are mental health professionals. The presenting problem was twofold. Following a decline in her husband's health, Mrs. D was experiencing symptoms of severe anxiety. She had difficulty sleeping and eating, exhibited nervous, hyperactive behavior, and was making inappropriate demands on the time and attention of her children.

Psychosocial History. Mrs. D was a sprightly 75-year-old woman, still driving and accustomed to being very active in community social and volunteer activities. She described her first marriage, which had lasted for more than 40 years, in very positive terms. The marriage produced two very successful children. Her first husband died after a lengthy and debilitating illness. It was during this time that she first experienced severe anxiety symptoms.

She continually alluded to the extremely supportive behavior of her daughters during her husband's final illness. Almost as an afterthought, Mrs. D reported that during this same period, she was diagnosed with lymphatic cancer. She had to undergo prolonged, difficult chemotherapy and radiation treatments which resulted in apparent cure. Yet she only spoke feelingly when discussing the difficulties in arranging care for her husband during her own prolonged disability.

Mr. and Mrs. D met through their common activities at the local senior adult center. Mr. D had been an active and dynamic member and acknowledged leader of the senior adult community. At that time, Mr. D was married and caring for his mentally and physically impaired wife. Mrs. D had been impressed by his ability to care for his wife while maintaining his other activities and attracted by his uxorious qualities as a husband. They married about a year after Mr. D was widowed and both had high hopes for an active and happy second marriage. For a while, their hopes were realized.

From the beginning, relationships between the two family network systems were cordial, but not intimate. Mrs. D always felt that her husband's adult children and grandchildren were not considerate of the older couple. She related one incident which illustrates the underlying issues: financial concerns and inadequate bonding between the two family network systems. Early in the marriage, the couple purchased a new, four-door car in order to allow easy access to front and back seats for Mrs. D. Mr. D's adult children questioned both the need for a new car and the extra expense of the four-door model. These kinds of issues, while disturbing, remained a minor factor in the relationship. This uneasy truce broke down when Mr. D's health began to fail.

About a year after the wedding, Mr. D suffered a heart attack from which he never fully recovered. He lost a great deal of weight and became very frail. All of his volunteer commitments were terminated and his recreational and social activities were severely curtailed due to his inability to sustain even minimal physical activity. The couple's life-style was completely changed.

In spite of Mr. D's obvious frailty and deterioration, his children and grandchildren did not alter their relationship pattern with the older couple in any way. Mrs. D made repeated requests for shorter and more frequent visits, with no results. They continued to make infrequent and lengthy visits, and with obvious expectations to be fed and entertained when they came. In addition, they continued to expect financial and emotional support from their parent, without apparently being able to recognize the changed circumstances. Mrs. D could not understand or condone the attitudes of his adult children and grandchildren.

The crisis erupted when, in spite of the unencouraging interactions with his children, Mrs. D made the request that they provide her with respite care so that she could visit one of her daughters, who resided in another state. She was rebuffed and turned to her own daughters, demanding not only emotional support, but respite care. She was caught in an angry internal conflict when her children refused to cooperate.

Diagnosis. In a remarkably short time, Mrs. D had presented the major issues that were troubling her: revived anxiety over her own health; fear of a prolonged period of spousal dependency;

ambivalence concerning her self-imposed ideals as a caregiver; conflict and confusion over the roles and expectations of the adult children and stepchildren in caregiving; disappointment that the dream of an active, interesting retired life-style was disappearing (for a second time); and finally, mourning for the loss of her dying spouse.

Mrs. D relied heavily on denial and projection to manage the emotions and feelings that were unacceptable to her and her anxieties about death and dying. For instance, her need to deny her fear of death was so powerful that she made no connection between her illness and her daughters' supportiveness during their father's final illness. She attributed all of their caring and helpfulness to their father's problems.

When asked what she would like to accomplish in psychotherapy, she requested medication for anxiety which had alleviated her symptoms in the past. Her recollection was that a psychiatrist gave her "pills" which took care of everything immediately. During the course of the treatment, she continually indicated an intolerance of painful feelings and expressed the wish or demand for them to go away. Her need for immediate relief of her symptoms and desire for control over her situation was so powerful that she approached a psychiatrist after the first counseling session in order to get "pills." She was predictably upset that they did not provide instantaneous relief.

Mr. D appeared tired and was silent unless responding to a direct question. He was apologetic that his illness was causing such trouble and hopeful that the counseling process would help the situation. He verbalized his feelings of dependence and inability to contribute to any solutions. His physical health precluded much physical or mental activity. While he had hopes that he would improve with time, he was unable to help her and was also unable to participate fully in psychotherapy sessions. Clearly, he had always been passive in family relationships and was unable and unwilling to try to change now. On the positive side, he exhibited real concern about his wife's well-being and understanding of her feelings and expressed willingness to cooperate with home health care and respite care plans so that his wife could have some freedom from caregiving responsibilities.

Finally, there were the issues of the extended family network systems. Financial concerns on the part of Mr. D's children had prompted only a token acceptance of the second Mrs. D into the family. They appeared to relate to her more as if she were paid help rather than their father's wife. Mr. D did not sanction any intervention with his children. Mrs. D's family apparently accepted the second marriage with less ambivalence; however, they were unwilling to pick up on caregiving responsibilities for their mother's husband. Their concern was for their mother and for their relationship with their mother. They were fearful that her anger and distress were so great that they would adversely affect Mrs. D's health and that her anger at his children would get permanently displaced on them. They had verbalized these feelings openly to their mother and had asked her to seek counseling.

Treatment. Because of Mr. D's health, the couple was only seen twice, for the first and last session. Mrs. D was seen individually for four sessions and she provided most of the psychosocial history. On this basis, it was agreed to work with Mrs. D to see what might be done about her anxiety symptoms. At the first individual meeting, the therapist asked Mrs. D what might help her feel better. She requested medication for anxiety as stated earlier. On learning that the therapist could not prescribe medication, she approached a doctor that day and got "pills." It was clear that Mrs. D was entering counseling reluctantly. In addition to seeking medication, she spoke at length about her two children, lauding their professional expertise, which she felt should preclude the need for her to speak to another mental health professional. She did not appear to be consciously aware of resentment toward her adult children for referring her to outside counseling, but made it clear that she felt abandoned in her need for emotional support and physical respite from nursing a sick spouse.

Since her resistance did not take the form of cancellations or inability to verbalize her problems, the issue was not addressed directly. Instead, focus was shifted to other times when Mrs. D had experienced severe anxiety. Mrs. D was provided with the opportunity to ventilate, sort out, and validate her feelings. The therapist focused Mrs. D on her feelings by commenting on the fears and anxiety that she must have experienced when both she and her first husband were desperately ill and how hard it must have been to need to be strong for both of them.

Major interpretive interventions occurred when the therapist pointed out how frightened and anxious feelings from the past seemed to have returned, perhaps due in part to similar circumstances. However, after the therapist noted how the similarity of the situations may have provoked severe anxiety from the past, the differences in the situation were underlined and emphasized. Mrs. D was not ill at the present time; she only feared that she might become ill. The adult children in this instance were not shared by both spouses (i.e., Mr. D was not the father of her daughters and, as such, had much less claim to her children's time and attention; conversely, she was not mother to Mr. D's children and, therefore, had little influence and authority to control their behavior and decisions). Furthermore, the differences in attitudes and reactions of Mr. D's children and her own children in a similar crisis were pointed out. It was further noted that Mr. D did not seem to want to change his relationships with his children. Mrs. D began to experience a remission of the more severe anxiety symptoms and the focus of the meetings changed to exploring alternate methods of acquiring some respite from caregiving.

A final interview was held with the couple, during which this information was shared with the husband. Mr. D confirmed his wish to maintain the current relationship style with his adult children and Mrs. D was able to validate his choice and still state that she needed some respite. Alternatives to family care were discussed and the couple was given information about other respite care resources in the community that might offer Mrs. D options so that she could plan a more active life-style while still providing the major share of caregiving for her spouse, a responsibility which she appeared to want. Mr. D was supportive of her plan to visit her daughter and to become more active in the community by herself, since he was unable to participate at this time. He was pleased with the outcome of our discussions.

Mrs. D however, terminated therapy with the last word. She judged the therapist to be "a nice and well-intentioned girl" and absolved the therapist and the therapeutic process from fault in that, "there was nothing to be done. . . . Not even the pills work like they used to."

At the time of this writing, Mrs. D is coping nicely. The symptoms of anxiety abated and she did manage to visit her child and became more active in the community. Before Mr. D died, she provided the lion's share of caregiving, and felt good about herself for meeting her own ideal. She is still involved in activities at the senior adult center and unresigned to the defection of the younger generation.

The Frail Elderly Family

With the great increase in human longevity, the frail, elderly family has emerged in large enough numbers to form a new family subgroup and constitutes a major responsibility for today's family network system. Most often, the frail elderly family consists of an elderly person alone or a married couple. At times, we may see other combinations of relatives or friends living together. The variables that define the frail elderly family are separate and independent residence and the need for partial or total custodial care. The continuum of care most often begins with the spouse (Getzel, 1982). Normally, the adult children will only offer or arrange for collateral care. Only in the case of the widowed or divorced elderly parent, does the family network system assume the full responsibility for caregiving.

The frail elderly are in the last stage of the life cycle. Thus, the salient psychological issues for the elderly individual or couple are dependency and death and dying (Neugarten, 1964). Individually or jointly, they are experiencing physical and mental decline at an ever-increasing rate and each assault on physical or mental health requires more recovery time and leaves additional permanent disabilities.

The elderly couple dealing with the acute or chronic illness of one of the marital partners faces major role changes. One of the couple becomes the primary caretaker as the other becomes progressively unable to assume normal and customary roles and functions. When one member of the couple becomes physically or mentally frail, the scope of the marital relationship begins to narrow, as the affected partner is unable to respond or participate fully in many aspects of the customary marital bond and the other partner finds him or herself more and more occupied with caregiving responsibilities. There is increasing isolation and inability to maintain family and social ties. Many issues—individual, marital, and family—are activated by the events and tasks inherent in this time of life and they place an enormous physical and emotional burden on all family members.

Caregiving may be especially difficult in certain circumstances; for example:

- If necessary role changes for the caregiver, the dependent person, or both are especially severe.
- If the caregiver was used to being dependent on the now-dependent individual (role reversal). For example, if the wife relied on her husband to make decisions and take care of normal family business, and perhaps expected him to indulge her, but now must provide care for a spouse who is no longer capable of making decisions for the family and can no longer be the uxorious husband.
- When the dependent person's sense of self-worth is particularly reli-

ant on physical prowess and/or a sense of control (e.g., a person who excelled at sports who is now confined to a wheelchair).

• When the caregiver is used to being active outside the home and having interests and activities separate from the dependent spouse and is unable to adjust to the demands of caregiving.

The Older Couple as Caretakers of Elderly Parents

Caring for the older generation is not a new role for family systems. It is the issues involved in caregiving that are new, because of all the changes in structure and function that have occurred in the individual and the family unit, over time and in the presence of environmental and social stressors.

Fifty years ago, elderly individuals were 60 years old. The course of terminal illness and dependency was very short. The extended family structure allowed caregiving responsibilities to be parceled out among many caregivers, and since the different generations of the family either lived in the same home, or in the same immediate neighborhood, the logistics of providing hands-on care were not only possible, but relatively simple as well.

Today, when we are referring to the elderly, we are generally discussing individuals over the age of 75 and who may well live into their 90s. Thus, some level of progressive physical or mental frailty may be present for as long as 20 years. Furthermore, as the life span lengthens, a significant number of families are beginning to consist of four generations, and often two generations of this family configuration are in the retirement years. Recent data show that one out of three persons over the age of 65 has a living parent (A. A. R. P. & U. S. Dept. of Health and Human Resources, 1986). Thus, one-third of adult child caregivers are aged themselves, although caregivers are usually in late middle age.

Often, just as elderly family members are beginning to experience the more serious forms of decline and need help in order to maintain independence and quality of life, their adult children are facing their own problems with the climacteric, retirement, and/or ill health. A further complication occurs since the dependency and decline of elderly family members tends to activate personal fears of aging in the caregivers. When this occurs, there is a direct effect on the ability of the family network system to provide the necessary care and services to the frail elderly generation. The objectivity necessary for assessment is lost, and decisions are based on irrational fears rather than on the realities of the situation. For instance, children who have physical problems such as heart disease, may be unable to see the inability of a parent to function due to a physical condition, and consequently be unable to either provide the necessary home health care or arrange for placement.

The quality of the relationship between the caregiver and the dependent person is another variable affecting appropriate caregiving. If the relationship has been negative or there are separation-individuation issues, the caregiver may not be able to recognize the needs of the frail individual. Worse, there may be neglect, exploitation, or abuse. In such instances, protective services and/or placement in a nursing home may become a necessity.

In general, there are fewer family members with whom to share any burdens, and often, all possible caregivers are still in the work force, even those over age 65. Thus, the caregiving generation may be depleted of the financial, physical, or emotional resources necessary to provide care for the older generation of the family. Modern medicine has improved human longevity but, sadly, created the side effect of a lengthy (perhaps as long as 15 or 20 years) period of partial or total dependency in old age, for which the aged individual, the family, and society are ill prepared. Even so, the elderly are usually not neglected and abandoned by the family network system to which they belong (Lebowitz, 1978). Families have found ways to interact with and activate friends and community resources to supply what they themselves are unable to provide. Today's family system is learning to connect their frail, elderly members with community resources, in the same way that they connect their children to community institutions. What has become a major issue between the generations arises when someone has lived past the time when they are "happy," i.e., when they can still find some pleasure, contentment, or interest in life. The provision of care and service may become equated with providing happiness and satisfaction in life in the minds of both the caregiver and the dependent, elderly person. But no amount of sensitive care from the family can imbue a life with pleasure and meaning. This expectation from either party can only lead to frustration and an unwillingness to provide and/or accept a care plan.

The family system continues to supply about 80% of hands-on care for their frail, elderly relatives (Lebowitz, 1978), but the difficulties and complexities of maintaining this family function are growing. We have only begun to understand the needs of caregivers, either spouses or adult children, when this kind of crisis becomes chronic and extends for lengthy periods. We do know that when the older couple is called on to function as caregivers for elderly parents, their capacity to perform effectively will depend on four issues:

- how well they are dealing with their own aging process
- the past and present relationship with the elderly parent
- the environmental stresses impacting the caregiving generation
- and the formal and informal resources available to the caregiving generation

CONCLUSIONS

Individuals and couples in the latter stages of the life cycle will face very serious problems, many of which are the by-product of reaching great age, and many of which were unknown even a generation ago. Beginning with early aging, when the mature couple begins to provide care for the generation that preceded them, as well as for the generation that will follow them, the caregiving generation begins to assume complicated and problematic functions in the family network system as they provide a launching platform to propel the younger generation into independent life functioning and ease the elderly generation through the stages of increasing dependency and, finally, out of life. No other time in the life cycle presents so many physical and social challenges. Problems are magnified and grow more complicated with the passage of time, the process of aging, and the prevailing social values which stress achievement, success, and productivity, every one of which is antithetical to the realities of old age. It is not difficult to see why we appear to have so much trouble defining aging and relating to the elderly. The older person, at times, may appear to be an unwanted member in a society that he has helped to create, but in which he can no longer participate.

Yet older individuals often seem to possess sufficient emotional resources to enable them to integrate their lives. Because of the aging and death phobia in our society, the strengths and contributions of older people to their family network system and society (i.e., wisdom, experience, financial power, etc.), are often underrated or even unrecognized. They serve as important role models in the family network system, demonstrating the process and the realities of growing old. In an increasingly alienated society that overvalues material possessions, they symbolize roots for the generations following them and they model another crucial asset: that the quantity and quality of what a person receives is not as important as whether he thinks it is enough. Furthermore, they represent social flexibility as outmoded roles are revised or discarded, and new roles for older family members are emerging all the time. It is clear that the older person's place in the family, though much changed, is far more important than is generally assumed—and he or she is as affected by family dynamics as is the younger generation.

3

The Mature-Stage Marriage: Definition and Issues

While couples and families in the latter stages of the life cycle have great strengths, they also have very serious problems, which are magnified and grow more complicated with the passage of time, the process of aging and prevailing social values. Older Americans, adopting the values and expectations of the general population, and being heavily impacted by recent changes in the family, have come to expect and need the marital relationship to provide a major share of life satisfactions. Direct observation of older couples in marital counseling suggests that older couples share the same marital concerns and problems that plague couples of any age. They are worried about communication, the balance of marital power, economic issues, and sexuality. Indeed, these issues appear to need renegotiation regularly throughout the family life cycle. However, in addition to dealing with normal marital issues, older couples are dealing with the inevitable social, biological, and psychological changes of growing old and the development tasks of the latter stages of the family life cycle. Engagement with these tasks is the determining factor in defining the mature-stage marriage.

THE MATURE-STAGE MARRIAGE DEFINED

While fully half the average family life cycle now occurs in the latter developmental stages, the nature of the marital process and the marital bond during late life has not been well studied.

Neither the age of the partners nor the duration of the marital bond is a reliable or definitive criterion of the mature-stage marriage or of marital success. Certainly, a marriage of many years suggests that the partners have worked out a marital balance that is satisfactory to them, and have had some experience and success with earlier stage developmental tasks. But serious disruptions can occur when the couple is faced with the process of aging. Rather, duration is only an indicator that the marital couple is probably dealing with mature-stage marital issues.

At the outset of the latter stages of the family life cycle (usually referred to as middle adulthood), the mature-stage marriage is characterized by the return to the marital dyad. Children are adolescents or young adults, gone from, or in the process of leaving, the parental home. There is an awareness that oneself and one's spouse are no longer young and beautiful and are nearer to a personal confrontation with the negative aspects of the aging process. This is the phase in the life cycle when divorce and remarriage may be sought as solutions, as though the remarriage will result in rejuvenation.

The wife is dealing with menopausal changes and the husband with the male climacteric. Both processes have physiological and psychological impact. Hormonal imbalance can lead to physical distress and may have considerable impact on the marriage as well. The parents of the middle-adult couple are reaching the end of their lives. Therefore, in addition to the secondary grief process associated with the loss of youth, one or more of the spouses may be in mourning for his or her own parents. This process includes the reactivation of the separation anxiety which the finality of death imposes and the anxiety at the realization that they have reached the final stage of life themselves.

The last phase of the family life cycle finds the marital partners alone and the breadwinner no longer working. The loss of vocational role and the financial decline of retirement are important losses to the sense of self-esteem. Mourning for social role changes will result not only from the death of important others, but also for the changes in social status and activities. Physical decline now accelerates and, ultimately, only the husband or the wife is the survivor.

The specific criterion defining the mature-stage marriage is the presence of the trigger events that begin the process of engagement with the mature-stage marital tasks. Thus, a second marriage after the age of 45 will from the outset have some issues and elements characteristic of the mature-stage marriage, even though the duration of the marital bond for these marital partners is brand new.

The May-December marital structure (i.e., spouses widely divergent in age) will also have elements of the mature stage marriage, since at least one of the marital partners is likely to be in the latter developmental stages of life. Such a structure presents one of the more complicated and interesting sets of dynamics and developmental issues in marital counseling. In rare cases, marital couples, engaged in much earlier stages of the family life cycle, will have to deal with mature-stage marital tasks, when terminal illness or death occurs to either spouse, out of sequence (before normally expectable).

TRIGGER EVENTS THAT DEFINE THE MATURE-STAGE MARRIAGE

It has been suggested that developmental tasks are cyclical in nature and require new resolution at each stage of the life cycle (Brennan & Weick, 1981). Another way to view these tasks is in terms of the constant couplings and uncouplings that signal the need for developmental growth and change and herald a new stage in the life cycle. Biological, social, and psychological events always occur to mark the beginning of the change. Physical decline, social role changes, and psychological and personality changes are all marker events that are characteristic of the mature-stage marriage.

Psychological and Personality Changes

As the individual grows older, there are normal changes in mental functioning associated with biological aging. The mental processes slow fractionally and there is some loss of ability to recall present and immediate past events. There is some speculation as to the causes of this memory loss. One of the more interesting hypotheses is that the memory loss is an escape from the unpleasant reality of being old.

The personality remains remarkably stable, but nonetheless, evidence has accumulated indicating that systematic and measurable changes occur in the second half of life. Men seem to become more receptive to affiliative and nurturant promptings and women more responsive toward, and less guilty about, aggressive and egocentric impulses. In both sexes, older people move toward more egocentric, self-preoccupied positions and attend increasingly to the control and satisfaction of personal needs. With the change from active to passive modes of mastering the environment, there is also a movement of energy away from an outer-world to an inner-world orientation.

Physical Decline in Early Aging

The awareness of physical decline begins with an awareness of a change in looks. Wrinkles begin to be apparent, and hair thins and greys. Teeth will probably need considerable repair and/or replacement. In general, muscles and skin lose tone and firmness. All of these changes account for "looking old." Actual loss of function is minor, but the emotional reaction to the change is major. These changes in appearance are accompanied by the hormonal shifts of the climacteric. The combined impact is severe enough that the individual's sense of time is shifted and is now measured from death rather than birth. This altered sense of time triggers the evaluation and reassessment process of life goals, which is the crucial task of middle adulthood.

While the individual in middle adulthood may begin to experience some harbingers of more serious physical decline, such as high blood pressure, the likelihood is that major physical decline will only be experienced after the age of 70, or even 75. It is in late adulthood that chronic and debilitating conditions begin to appear with regularity. Physical health begins to occupy major emotional, physical, and financial investment, and the developmental tasks of late life are triggered.

Social Role Changes

It is the family and the relationships within the family, both past and present, that contribute most to an older person's sense of self-worth and accomplishment. Therefore the changes in family role for the older couple are crucial to the successful accomplishment of the tasks of both the mid-life and the late life developmental stages. The mature-stage marriage begins with the social role change that shifts emphasis from parental functioning to the marital dyad. Interest and capacity for nurturance find new outlets in providing care for the elderly generation of the family, and in an interest in social and civic activities.

The elderly generation of the family network system now requires more care. With increasing physical or mental frailty, a gradual role change takes place, in which the elderly parent becomes able to express dependence on the adult child and the adult child becomes able to accept that dependence. In the caretaking generation, this role shift has been termed "filial maturity" (Blenker, 1965). It represents a loss, both to the elderly parents and to their adult children.

In mid-life, role change often means an expansion and shifting of roles as the individual stretches for maximal achievement professionally and personally. A sense of social and civic responsibility is developed, in part as a response to the nurturing drive, but mainly as an adaptive mechanism to bolster self-esteem, to aid in preparation for retirement and finally to promote the acceptance of personal mortality when death becomes imminent.

Grandparenting

One of the most rewarding and exciting role expansions the older couple has the opportunity to share is that of grandparenting. This experience can be rejuvenating for the mature-stage marriage. With the evidence of a job well done, one can parent adult children and grandchildren on a limited basis, leaving when the difficulties become too much to bear or when one is simply no longer interested. Grandparents do not feel responsible for mistakes or lack of performance. In fact, they may have the opportunity to do better the second time around. The role is immensely gratifying, and even when there is minimal intergenerational interaction, the existence of grandchildren signals to the older generation the continuity of a future they have participated in creating, even if they will not be there to see it. It is another aid in the process of accepting personal mortality.

Thus, the task in the early phase of the mature-stage marriage is to let adult children go in a creative sense, to build their own lives and families, separate from the family of origin, while making a place in which the family of origin can participate. During this period, the normal three-generation family (i.e., adult children, the caretaking generation and the elderly generation of the family) remain in relatively stable relationships and relate in an equality mode. Adult children will be assuming more and more caretaking responsibilities as they have children of their own, and the caretaking generation will be coping with late life developmental issues as they move closer to the position of the elderly generation in the extended family network.

With longevity and gains in good health, mid-life is extended from the 40s to the 70s and can be the apogee of the human life cycle, when the personal, physical, emotional, mental, social, professional, and financial resources converge to create a cooperative zenith of functioning not to be achieved separately. It appears to be a flowering before the repose of late life.

For couples in the final phase of the mature-stage marriage, the core issues are control, autonomy, dependency, and death. These issues play out in the marriage and the community, and at this stage of life return with renewed vigor to the extended family network, which can consist of four and even five generations in a family. This is a circular pattern that can impact on the couple in the early phase of the mature-stage marriage, as elderly parents request and require a significant portion of the couple's emotional, physical, and financial resources. Characteristic of the final phase in mature stage marriages is the process of role reduction. Family roles become increasingly important and may even become, finally, the only social role system to which the individual still belongs. The major developmental task for the marital partners is the integration of loss, the reinvestment of the marital relationship on a level commensurate with the realistic capacities for functioning of both marital partners, and coping with the physical decline and death of the spouse and one's self.

Retirement

The major role reduction for the late mature-stage couple is retirement. Retirement signals major attachment and separation issues involving vital role and life-style changes which impact enormously on self-worth. Preparation, which aids in staving off the worst pangs and effects of retirement, can begin long before the actual event. But many people seem "caught by surprise." These individuals have a difficult time identifying with the positive aspects of aging and retirement and are likely to cause problems not only for themselves, but also for the extended family network and, most particularly, for the caretaking generation.

The reasons for their resistance are not difficult to fathom. Status maintenance and financial considerations are paramount, but the normal resistance to change and the intrinsic nature and value of work play a very important part as well. Society, or the organization, and the person do not always agree when retirement should occur. Age is most often the indicator used to determine retirement, even though it is only a fair indicator of readiness. It fails to identify the younger adult who is psychologically and economically ready to retire and the vigorous older person who in his and his company's judgment is capable of continuing to work.

For most, however, it is not the absence of work that is the only, or even the major, problem confronting the new retiree. It is the disruption of life patterns and the necessity of establishing new ones, which create the most difficulty, even for those individuals with the most positive attitude toward retirement. Negative attitudes in the society about aging and retirement complicate the process of establishing new patterns. Leisure is a state of mind rather than an activity. Hannah Arendt (1959, p. 385) traced the evolution of this cultural ideal from the ancient Greeks, who could appreciate a leisure society, to modern Western man, to whom work is the sole raison d'être and leisure is only the absence of work. In our society, if an activity is for profit, it is defined as work; if it is for pleasure, it is leisure. Establishing new patterns is a slow and difficult process, at best. The choice is not between activity and inactivity, but between kinds and levels of activity. The necessary shifts in roles and activities can be accomplished only through process of trial and error, until the selection process produces satisfaction and the continued growth and stimulation that makes each person's life interesting and rewarding.

Physical Decline in Late Aging and Death

At this time, acute and chronic physical problems lead to further role constriction, as the individual loses the physical ability to participate in activities and events. With increased longevity, human beings are suffering from chronic, debilitating conditions. While not life-threatening, they significantly reduce the quality of life. Arthritis is an excellent example of such a condition. Other diseases are life-threatening, but at some nebulous time in the future. Diseases such as high blood pressure are an anxious reminder that things are happening within the body, out of sight, over which there is little control. Further role constriction results with the demise of friends, neighbors, and the people and institutions that make up the social support system of the individual. And finally, the most wrenching role constriction occurs with the loss of the spousal role.

In summary, these trigger events signal the advent of *the mature-stage marital developmental tasks*:

- resolving conflicts and stabilizing the marriage for the long haul
- supporting and enhancing each other's struggle for productivity and fulfillment in the face of threats of aging
- redefining intimacy and interactional patterns as the couple spends more actual time together and physical space and roles may be violated
- setting new goals that are appropriate and attainable
- redefining roles within the marital dyad, the extended family network, and society in order to provide a sense of meaning and productivity to retirement
- validating all stages of the marriage

- having the capacity to live together as a couple (appropriate attachment) for as long as time and health permit without being unduly concerned about the illness or death of either spouse in the future
- having the capacity to mourn self losses, spouse losses, and marital losses and still be together in a meaningful way
- having the capacity to nurture in new and creative ways, as physical problems may limit sexual expression and other physical or mental impairment may require more care from one spouse with limited ability of the other to reciprocate
- having the capacity to let go when one member of the couple is unable to function in the marriage any longer or death intervenes
- having the capacity to view oneself as an individual with a meaningful life, which is separate from the spouse and which will continue if illness or death enforce separation.

Basically, these tasks revolve around stabilizing the marriage; keeping affects within bearable limits during sudden life crises (e.g., following a death); restoring emotional balance by postponing or channeling sudden increases or decreases in biological drives; mastering changes in self-image (those for the better as well as those for the worse); handling unresolvable conflicts with people, living or dead, whom one cannot bear to leave; and surviving major conflicts with conscience (e.g., placing a spouse in a nursing home).

MARITAL ISSUES IN THE MATURE-STAGE MARRIAGE

Each partner brings to the marital relationship not only his or her usual pattern of attempting to satisfy personal needs, but also his or her way of reacting to needs in the other person. We recognize that choice of marital partner may represent many different motivations and that each partner takes into marriage some unresolved conflicts and needs from childhood. When the marriage relationship fails to afford satisfaction of needs, or fails to meet them in ways to which the individual has been accustomed, conflicts develop, and a destructive spiral may be set in motion. Frustration, resentment, and the breakdown of meaningful communication destroy the ability to support each partner's personal identity and fail to alleviate anxiety about self, a central purpose in the marital bond. When this function fails, the marriage is in jeopardy.

The developmental life cycle of the individual and the family can also produce unique expressions of marital conflict. A major source of developmental conflict occurs when there is incongruence between the individual life cycle and the family life cycle. The tasks that occupy the energy of the family may not be the tasks that occupy one or more of the individuals in the family. This may lead the members of the family to the conclusion that the relationship is failing. Then too, struggling with their own developmental tasks, adult family members may have little time or energy to invest in helping aging parents whose inability to cope with the problems of aging creates anxiety and depression in both generations. Overwhelmed by their inability to meet the demands made on them by dependent family members, the entire family experiences a state of crisis. Often, this is expressed in marital conflict. Additionally, new and reactivated conflicts may be caused by changes in life circumstances, such as retirement. And regression to childhood roles awakens the unresolved conflicts of the past and reactivates prior psychopathological patterns.

These basic premises hold true at all stages of the family life cycle. What is often confounding in the mature-stage marriage is that marital patterns that were successful in earlier stages of the family life cycle may fail the partners when they are faced with the events of middle and late life. Such failure has complex sources and roots.

Marital Compatibility Issues

At the outset of the mature-stage marriage, marital conflict tends to arise from different rates and directions of emotional growth. Concerns about the loss of youth may lead to depression and/or acting out and intimacy is threatened by aging and by the boredom inherent in a secure and stable relationship. Conflict often increases when children leave and the level of intimacy increases or decreases. Toward the end of the middle adulthood phase of the mature-stage marriage, the marital bond is vulnerable to nonrelational crises such as illness, death, job change, and sudden shifts in role relationships (i.e., filial maturity, described earlier in this chapter).

When children leave home, the parental partners have time to reflect on their marriage. Selection of a partner 25 or 30 years ago may have been dictated by needs based upon regression and fixation, a defensive arrangement, or other nongrowth-promoting and adaptive features in the personality. Those needs may have changed over the years, to the extent that the marital partner is no longer compatible in terms of self-image, personal and marital goals, capacity for emotional and sexual intimacy, interests and activities, personal values and attitudes, and professional and financial expectations of achievement for self, the partner, and the marriage.

Bringing up children may have masked a growing incompatibility through the absorption of the couple's time and energy, and may also have afforded both husband and wife adequate fulfillment of their individual needs. Or, it may have provided the opportunity to escape from an intimate relationship with each other. When these compensations that may have camouflaged the deficiencies in the marital relationship are gone, open conflict can erupt.

For many other reasons, children provide powerful motivations to maintain the marital relationship past the time when it meets the partner's needs for intimacy. Both partners may feel the primary responsibility to raise children before feeling free to pursue self-gratification. Women may feel that their parenting function would be seriously compromised by the demands of working and single-parenting. Men have also maintained marital relationships out of unwillingness to lose primary contact with their children. One or both may feel unwilling to deal with the stepparenting issues of remarriage.

Financial considerations may also bind a couple together. Women may feel incapable of providing financially for children and themselves alone, and men may feel unable to support two households. And, of course, either or both may be unwilling to split the family assets. Such marriages have basic deficiencies in caring and intimacy that leave both of the partners extremely vulnerable to the crises of middle and late life.

The expression of sexual behavior can be an important compatibility issue for older couples. While other cultures provide for and expect continual sexual activity in older adults, ours is a culture that considers sexual outlets unacceptable and unimportant for older people, especially for those in late life. Such attitudes reinforce repression and produce guilt and anxiety about sexual drives in later life. These feelings tend to inhibit individuals from asking questions about normal sexual changes during the aging process. According to William Masters and Virginia Johnson (1966), ignorance is one of the greatest deterrents to effective sexual functioning in all ages, but it has been most damaging to older people. Research has revealed some significant information concerning the expression of sexuality in the latter stages of the life cycle. There is a potential for decline of sexual activity and potency due to biological changes in the aging process. However, this is no indication that desire is nonexistent. As in younger men, impotence in older men results from fear of failure; however, fear of failure in the older man is often based on misinformation about normal sexual functioning at this stage of life. Women appear to be capable of sexual response in later years to a greater extent than men, and are affected more by the capacity or lack of partners.

The rate of sexual activity decreases little, if at all, in the middle-adult stage of the life cycle. And although decreasing, it is still present in 70% of males at age 70. From the age of 70 to 75 there seems to be a more serious decline; only 50% of men are still sexually active. However, men who have been sexually active for much of their lives may expect, in the absence of serious disease process, to maintain interest and activity, even into very old age. For women, the same is true, except that they are more likely to cease activity due to loss of a suitable partner than any other reason. The consensus of the experts is that regularity of sexual activity is the essential factor in maintaining an effective performance.

There are important changes, however. Responsiveness to sexual stimuli declines with age. Men experience a decrease in the vigor of ejaculation, the frequency and strength of erection diminishes, and a longer period is required to reach climax. The alteration in function may be an advantage rather than a problem. However, in many instances, older men, when confronted with repeated erectile slow-down, are apt to jump to the conclusion that they have become impotent and that this is an unavoidable concomitant of the aging process.

Whereas the decline in the activity of the male sex gland is so gradual as to be almost imperceptible, in the female it is more abrupt and results in the so-called change of life. Physical changes occur in the sexual organs of women also. The lining of the vagina thins and there is diminishment of lubrication. The vagina and the labia majora also shrink. All of these changes may cause painful intercourse, but they are easily treated, and a woman is more or less capable of and receptive to sexual activity throughout her entire life span. But an aging woman does need to feel attractive and wanted by her husband. Consequently, she may interpret her husband's waning interests and energies as a personal rejection. When these two reactions—the man's fear of impotence and the woman's feeling of being rejected—occur and remain unspoken, the relationship is likely to deteriorate drastically (Sander, 1976).

While the expression of sexual drive has lost its primary urgency for older people, it remains a very important area of marital functioning. Sexual problems figure heavily in the majority of marital counseling cases with older couples. Although sexual incompatibility is rarely cited as a presenting problem, it often surfaces as a marital issue after counseling has begun.

THE PSYCHODYNAMIC EFFECTS OF THE AGING PROCESS ON MARITAL FUNCTIONING

As the aging process continues to unfold normally throughout the human life cycle, the human organism becomes more vulnerable, biologically and psychodynamically. Normal life events, such as deaths, retirement, and social role change accelerate in pace and challenge the psychodynamic adaptive mechanisms and defenses. Narcissistic injury, depression, and anxiety are common complaints among older people and increase dramatically as the aging process continues into the final stage of life. These problems are further complicated by the pattern changes, values, and the ethical conundrums of our modern society.

Narcissistic Injury in Aging

Otto Kernberg (1975) pointed out that aging brings into relief narcissistic problems which the person, while younger, had been able to manage. The confrontation of the physical, emotional, and social accompaniments of aging with the grandiose self can be devastating to the person and may easily lead to collapse. Sophie Loewenstein, in her article, "An Overview of the Concept of Narcissism" (1977), quotes an unpublished play about Hemingway by Frederic Hunter, in which the underlying theme is Hemingway's narcissism. The play describes how his narcissism—a driving, creative force in his younger years—increasingly creates shadows of grandiose coercion over his life, until we meet the old man, unable to tolerate his declining talent and public criticism and sinking into paranoia, alcoholism, and eventually suicide.

While Hemingway's example is extreme, there is no question that in the normal process of aging, humans suffer ever-increasing narcissistic injury. Recognition, self-affirmation, power, and self-esteem are the basic themes of human existence, and all of these themes are undergoing decline, change, or attack. Individuals who have never felt secure, accepted, and appreciated for themselves, and have never been allowed some control and initiative over their lives will probably have a damaged self-image and consequently will experience pathological narcissistic feelings. Fenichel (1945) described the role of narcissism in depression, in the person who is fixated on the state where his self-esteem is regulated by "external supplies." This person will have an inordinate need to be loved and consequently, will make excessive demands on love objects. In the attempt to maintain desperately needed supplies, such individuals exhibit behavior patterns that may further alienate love objects. Frustration tolerance is low, and submission, manipulation, coercion, demands, and placation are commonly used coping strategies. With aging, their ability to obtain supplies may be seriously compromised, and family and social relationships can be damaged, leading to significant isolation. More serious and debilitating consequences are alcoholism, hypochondriasis, and/or severe depression.

For everyone, the ability to fend off narcissistic injury declines during the aging process as the number and rate of internal and external losses increases.

Depression in the Aging Process

Depression is a serious emotional problem among older people and is directly related to the experience of loss, both internal and external. In fact, the major developmental task of late life is the integration of loss. In mid-life, losses are apt to be internal, such as the loss of ideals or hopes of attainment. In the elderly, external losses, such as the death of a friend, are more apt to produce depression. One of the major losses is the death of a spouse, which is a profoundly difficult event with which to cope. It is a multifaceted loss—a loss of companion, sexual partner, provider, homemaker, and so forth. Painful as it may be, such functions are replaceable, and it is the experience of internal loss that involves the "work" of mourning. However, as the rate and number of losses increase, it becomes more difficult to complete the uncomplicated mourning process that will lead to replacement. Eventually, the ability to mourn may be compromised and mourning will take a pathological route, expressed in hypochondriasis and continual depression.

Verwoerdt (1976) connected the experience of a neurotic or reactive depression of late life to mid-life crises. He noted an "involutional grief reaction" secondary to failure to attain ideals, realization of one's transience, relinquishing illusions of perennial progress, and other disillusionments.

For depression-prone older individuals, normal events are considered a personal defeat. They have difficulty coming to terms with physical decline, disease and death since they blame themselves for these events. Both normal and abnormal depressions in the older populations account for the significantly higher rate of depression among the older population.

Anxiety

Attachment concepts can be useful in understanding every stage of the life cycle. Circumstances that interfere with the establishment or continuation of human attachments can have serious consequences for the individual at any time in life. Impaired or broken attachment relationships have been related to marital problems, depression, and suicide in late life.

The normal anxiety that accompanies severe illness, losses, and deaths together with the prospect of one's own demise, can lead to what has been referred to as separation anxiety or attachment anxiety. In fact, the threat of separation is contained in practically every dysfunctional family transaction. Today, not only the finality of death provokes such anxiety. The prevalence of mental impairment has led to particularly poignant manifestations of attachment issues.

Attachment anxiety manifests itself through a clinging relationship and behavior that keeps partners in close proximity to each other, even when this is accompanied by considerable friction. Less obvious than clinging or proximity-seeking behavior are the various reactions to heightened attachment needs, usually expressed in exaggerated independence or retaliatory behavior. Furthermore, alcohol is often used by older individuals as a medicinal drug to counter anxiety and as a sedative. However expressed, attachment anxiety can produce considerable difficulties in the mature-stage marriage.

Patterns and Roles

Developmental change inevitably brings the disruption of life-style patterns and roles (Offer & Sabshin, 1984), for which we have little education and less preparation. Furthermore, we have ambivalent role models and scarce information for the role changes that accompany the latter stages of the life cycle. Large corporations are beginning to offer cushioning experiences, such as in-service training, practicums, part-time work experience, retirement seminars, voluntary activities that are integrated into the job description, and counseling, when indicated. However, at present these opportunities are rare and do not reach the majority of individuals.

The role changes associated with aging are probably more upsetting than the role reduction that occurs in the late life stage. In our society, roles are instrumental (i.e., geared toward getting tasks accomplished) or socioemotional (i.e., geared toward building relationship bonds) (Neugarten, 1970). Men tend to learn the skills associated with instrumental roles, and women, the skills of the socioemotional role. In the workplace, roles are increasingly instrumentally oriented until retirement, at which point roles abruptly change to the socioemotional ones (those that are associated with the female). Men may suffer further blows to the ego if their role is too strongly identified with the feminine. For instance, a man may be unable to channel energy into cooking or shopping if he too rigidly interprets such activities as female tasks.

With old age comes a significant decline in the number of groups of which one is a member (Sze, 1975). Accompanying the decline in groups is the decline in roles that an individual plays, such as religious, community, political, or social (friendship) roles. Often the family is the sole group to which the elderly individual belongs, and even this group is diminished in size in most cases and in too many others, may even be nonexistent. Group role (including the marital and family roles) and membership give support, define behavior, and bolster morale. The social functions of the group make it easier for society and its members to solve the crucial problems associated with man as a biological and social animal. Thus, the changes and declines in role are a profoundly upsetting event in the aging process, and to offset them the individual must make a major effort.

Along with role change is the disruption of family and individual life patterns. The dilemma for older couples often centers around the return to school for professional education or the return to work on the part of the wife, and the fact that new values may not be equally well integrated by both members of the couple.

The return to school or work often leads to overload and networking difficulties caused by the squeeze on private time, which, in turn, leads to limitations on family and friendship time. Serious role change and role cycling (referring to the shifting function of role from one member of the family to the other) dilemmas occur with great frequency. Guilt and identity confusion may be another consequence of the discrepancy between the theories of sexual and professional equality and childhood socialization. Later, loss of role and status that occurs with unmet expectations in career and, eventually, retirement, can lead to other problems with self-esteem.

Values, Attitudes, and Fears

Beginning with middle age, and mounting with increasing age, the prevailing values in society become alienated and create great stresses and problems in self-worth and identity. Achievement, work, efficiency, progress, external conformity, science, and rationality are all prevailing values that are antithetical to aging.

Blazer (1982) has stated that, "Personality characteristics, such as independence and autonomy, which once enabled individuals to master self and environment or gain prestige in early and middle life, may prevent adaptation in later years" (p. 67). Maturity has been defined as the passive acceptance of painful and inevitable situations antithetical to societal values. Furthermore, we are a society that regards grieving as abnormal and finds little value in being alone. People who choose to live alone often find themselves socially penalized. Thus, fear of loneliness may keep older couples together and often leads to second marriages late in life.

Older couples may also run into trouble over values that taught them to sacrifice self to the marriage. In the past, individuals had different personal boundaries and fears of abandonment than those that prevail currently. These values conflict with new values in marriage.

Ethical Issues

The advances in technology, medicine, and public health that have led to increases in longevity and the large numbers of the elderly in our population have also created ethical issues that impact heavily on the older population (Neugarten, 1970). These issues concern the right to die; quantity and methods of treatment in terminal illness; caretaking for dependent family members, which may stretch into many years (especially when related to mental impairments such as Alzheimer's Disease); nursing home placement; and the financial concerns raised by costs of care for dependent family members. One study, which looked at 300 applications for counseling involving older couples, cited the institutionalization of a spouse, the acceptance of terminal illness, and sexual, social, and interdependence needs as the major sources of requests for individual and marital counseling (Werner & Varner, 1983).

Older couples today face ethical issues that were unheard of only a generation ago. Today, we are able to keep people alive, at times with little or no quality of life. Our legal system ties the hands of the medical community and the family as well. Adult children who try to provide care for dependent parents can find themselves in a nightmare of 24-hour daily obligation with little or no family or community support.

Treatment for serious diseases such as cancer, heart disease, and strokes can be more debilitating than the disease they are designed to treat. Cancer patients often reach the point of refusing further treatment, since the side effects are so physically and emotionally destructive. The tremendous stresses undergone by spouses, children, and other family members, who are an important support structure during the aggressive treatment of physical or mental impairment, are often ignored, unless they specifically request intervention.

Many of the elderly find themselves confined to psychiatric wards due to the behavioral and emotional problems caused by the interactions of many different medications. The decisions that must be made, in these and similar situations, can cause rifts that reverberate throughout the generations of a family, and account for a great number of requests for individual or marital counseling, both from the elderly parental generation and their adult children, who need help in making caretaking decisions, in dealing with disagreements about the needs and resources of caretaking, or in dealing directly with marital problems that are caused by, or directly related to, the caretaking needs of the elderly generation.

CONCLUSIONS

There are recurrent themes in psychotherapy with older clients. Some are caused by the crises of growing older and are unique to a particular age group, whereas others are similar to those presented by adult clients of all ages. These issues, which may have great poignancy when presented by elderly clients with limited options, concern growing old, conflicts with children, and conflicts with spouse.

The decade of the 50s inaugurates a period in the life cycle when there is unique developmental work to be done. In the youth of our aging process, the major developmental task is to clarify, deepen, and find use for what one has already learned in a lifetime of adapting. At the end of the aging continuum, the elderly must teach themselves to conserve their strength and resources when necessary and to adjust, in the best sense, to those changes and losses that occur as a part of aging. At no other time in life are the stresses and losses so numerous, so pervasive, so sequential—in a word, normal. The adaptive capacities are challenged continually during the latter stages of the aging process. The danger is that the losses can so easily become the major or even the sole focus of life, so that the gains and the options may be obscured or lost. Time is really the only luxury, and now there is time: time to pay attention to self, time to spend on interests and hobbies, time to develop new ones, time to see the world (externally and internally), and time to get to know one's family and see the future in grandchildren.

The challenge facing older couples and individuals is complicated and multifaceted. The contract between the client and the practitioner is to create together an arena of options, while supporting and allowing the dignity and the authenticity of the struggle with conflicting needs, images, and expectations (Weick, 1983). At times, the complexities of the issues and the task are intimidating; indeed, the literature has questioned whether the practitioner has the ability or the client has the emotional and financial resources, life expectations, and capacity to change to warrant the investment in time required by psychotherapy. Erik Erikson (1964) has the best answer to that hypothesis:

> Any span of the cycle lived without vigorous meaning, at the beginning, in the middle, or at the end, endangers the sense of life and the meaning of death in all whose life stages are intertwined. (p. 133)

4

A Developmental Marital Counseling Model for Older Couples

Through time, the marital relationship assumes increasing importance to the aging individual. Once the children are launched in life, the marital relationship once more dominates family life for the older couple and, especially among the elderly, is often the most important relationship left to both partners. Furthermore, during the last stages in the life cycle, self-esteem is under attack from many sources. A number of studies have demonstrated the link between marital satisfaction and self-esteem. And the link between self-esteem and emotional well-being is evident. Thus, a strong marital counseling component would appear to be an indispensable element of quality mental health service to the aged. Yet, in spite of the demonstrable need and the obvious benefits, the problems of older couples are only recently beginning to attract the attention of mental health professionals. Consequently, the development of marital counseling models and techniques which address the special needs and issues of couples in the mature-stage marriage have been neglected.

Probably this neglect is due to the widely underestimated motivation for change among older couples. The opposite is very often true. Motivation for change is high for many reasons: the long-term emotional investment, children and grandchildren, shared accumulated property and financial resources, familiarity, etc. The list is very long. But probably the greatest motivator of change in older people is the fear of loneliness if the marriage were to terminate. This is especially true for older women, as their chance of remarriage grows statistically slimmer with increasing age. Fear of loneliness can be more powerful than the need to maintain stubborn defenses that create friction and lead to mutual recriminations. This fear is often operating in instances of remarriage or sexual liaisons following a partner's death as well. And while a new sexual relationship can be a stabilizing and enriching one for the older person, adult children may be distressed about it, which may foster considerable feelings of guilt in the adult parent. In the long run, the level of commitment to an established relationship tends to be high, due to fears of loneliness and of the unknown.

The developmental marital therapy model presented here is a systems theory model (i.e., relationships and communication are understood within the framework of systems theory) specifically geared to the marital issues and problems experienced by older and elderly couples. The model melds life cycle and psychodynamic theories and postulates that role changes, physical modifications and decline, and retirement are the major life cycle events that impact on marriage at the late stages in the life cycle, and that the social, emotional, and biological events normal in the aging process trigger the initiation and execution of the developmental tasks of the mature-stage marriage.

Normal psychological events, such as introspection, reminiscence, and the life review, are incorporated into the body of the treatment model, both as therapeutic tools, and as therapeutic experience. Expectable life events involving loss and role changes are hypothesized as requiring a mourning process, however truncated, unusual or unrecognizable in form. Therefore, an important inclusion in the model is grief work. The model further hypothesizes that central to all of the individual and marital tasks at this stage of the life cycle is the search for meaning. This issue is addressed not only through the standard insight-oriented and supportive therapeutic techniques, but through a very active, task-oriented approach which facilitates the restructuring of role and task as life patterns and roles are seriously disrupted when children leave home, with the occurrence of physical changes and at retirement.

THE EVALUATION

Stage I of the treatment model evaluates the marriage in terms of the developmental stage and task of the individual partners and of the marital bond. The evaluation is accomplished by carefully exploring the presenting problem, any necessary medical or psycho-

TABLE 1. Developmental Marital Therapy Model for Older Couples

Stage I: Evaluation

1. Presenting problem
2. Any necessary psychological or medical testing
3. Beginning marital-life review
   Identify unresolved issues from the past
   Identify past developmental successes and failures (marital history)

Stage II: Treatment techniques

1. Ongoing marital-life review
   Reframe past developmental successes and failures
   Reframe unresolved issues and explore possibilities for resolution in
      the present
2. Insight-oriented therapy
   Use the marital life review and interpretation to bring to conscious-
      ness unresolved issues
   Through interpretation, produce personal and relational growth and
      adaptive change
3. Supportive therapy
   Strengthen mental functions that are acutely or chronically inade-
      quate to cope with the demands of the external world
   Help client explore "reality" (lending ego)
   Comfort, reassure, offer suggestions
4. Grief counseling
   Accept real losses (health, attractiveness, death)
   Clarify anticipated losses (fear of death, loss of income)

Stage III: Task- and action-oriented techniques

1. Promoting life-style changes
   Explore options
   Develop role flexibility
2. Identifying resources
   Financial
   Medical
   Other

Stage IV: Termination

1. Review of tasks
2. Review of individual strengths
3. Review of marital strengths

Reprinted with permission, from Wolinsky, "Marital Therapy with Older Couples," *Social Casework*, Oct. 1986. Published by Family Service America.

logical testing, and a process developed by the author called the
Marital Life Review. This process combines and directs the elements of the marital history and the life review process, while taking advantage of naturally occurring mental processes such as
reflection and reminiscence.

The Marital Life Review

In 1963, Robert Butler identified the life review process as an adaptive mechanism of the aging process. Reminiscence is the conscious, selective arm of remembering. The middle years of life (approximately age 50) are a period when introspection increases noticeably, and contemplation, reflection, and self-evaluation become characteristic forms of mental life. The reflection that takes place during middle age is probably the precursor of reminiscence in old age, and reminiscence is included in the life review process but is not analogous to it.

The life review process can be placed in the context of marital history. The taking of marital and family histories is routine in therapy. Giving history is a useful learning experience for the client and is usually accompanied by a sense of therapeutic accomplishment; it is also a major tool in facilitating separation-individuation by the marriage partners. The process can be further enhanced by reviewing pictures, artifacts, genograms, and marital memorabilia. The stage is then set with the unresolved issues from the past, and previous developmental successes and failures which provide valuable clues for structuring treatment techniques and goals.

TREATMENT TECHNIQUES

Insight-oriented Therapy

The ongoing marital life review uses naturally occurring mental processes such as reflection, reminiscence, and the ability to move thoughts from the subconscious to the conscious mind, which begins to increase with age. This process allows the therapist to use interpretive techniques, such as insight-oriented therapy, on unresolved issues from the past in a way that permits and enhances the possibilities for resolution in the present. Past successes and failures in developmental tasks can be reframed to encourage positive reintegration.

Supportive Therapy

The supportive therapy techniques of ego lending, helping the client explore reality, comforting, reassuring, and giving suggestions are especially valuable with older clients, especially those who have suffered multiple losses. Supportive therapy strengthens mental functions that are acutely or chronically inadequate to cope with the demands of the external world. Those losses may be as relatively benign as loss of personal attractiveness or as devastating as the death of a beloved spouse.

Grief Counseling

The amount of intense distress and emotional disturbance occasioned by loss is not well understood. There is a tendency to underestimate the distress and disability caused by grief reactions, as well as their duration. In our society, grief reactions are often viewed with suspicion, and it is not long before the mourner is exhorted to "get on with it" and assured that everything will be right again as soon as the mourner "stops feeling sorry for himself." Negative attitudes such as these often encourage people to bury their grief. Subsequently, they do not complete the tasks of mourning and never learn to accept their losses so they can move on and repopulate their world.

As people grow older, the ego gradually loses its capacity to refuel itself, and multiple losses limit opportunities for refueling. Stanley Cath (1965) used the term "depletion" to identify a state beyond depression. It is not unusual to see such people in a therapy program, which unfortunately at this time is usually an inpatient psychiatric setting. John Bowlby (1980) postulates that much psychiatric illness is an expression of pathological mourning. Thus, with the understanding that a major task of the mature-stage marriage is to integrate real and anticipated losses and with the realization that opportunities for mourning are limited and negatively reinforced in our society, it is incumbent to build a component of grief counseling into a marital therapy model for the mature-stage marriage.

The following case example illustrates how grief and losses can impact on a long-term, stable mature-stage marriage.

Case Example

Mrs. G entered counseling with the presenting problem of planning for her elderly mother. She was 59 years old, and had been married for 39 years. There were four grown children, all male, married and with children. The only daughter had died at age 14 of ovarian cancer. Mrs. G's father died very recently, and her mother was presently living with Mr. and Mrs. G.

It soon became evident that the major issues were marital and that the problems with her elderly mother had served as a catalyst to bring the marital issues to the surface. Although her husband had been requested to accompany her for counseling, he had refused to do so.

A marital history confirmed that the marriage was quite successful in many areas, particularly with regard to the sexual relationship. Mrs. G described her husband as extremely bright (he was a very successful professional), but rather spoiled and contentious in his behavior. She said that she had always resented his style of interaction, but had been compensated by their five children and thus, it had not seemed so important earlier in the marriage. She also reported difficulty in confronting him with her priorities, and never challenged him.

Ten years ago, her daughter had died of cancer. The same year, the three sons still at home had married. She felt that she had been left with her husband as a priority and, "I didn't want him as a priority." Mrs. G was very disappointed with her husband during her daughter's final illness and death. She felt that he had been unable to support either his daughter or his wife during the course of the disease, and subsequently, did not grieve with Mrs. G after the daughter's death. Mrs. G was unable to forgive her husband, and feels that the relationship changed at this time. She expresses the change in an unwillingness to cater to him or defer to his opinions, something he finds very difficult to accept.

The precipitating event that brought Mrs. G to counseling was the death of her father. Once again, she felt alone and abandoned during the process of caring for her dying father and, later, in her grief. Her husband had visited only once during the long final hospitalization and had appeared to be disgusted with the sights, smells, and sounds of his father-in-law's terminal illness. He expressed relief that it was all over. Mrs. G made a unilateral decision to bring her mother, who was incapable of living alone, to live with the G's. Mr. G was furious and there were frequent, serious arguments about this decision. Mrs. G states that she is prepared to get a divorce rather than put her mother in a nursing home. At the time of the application for counseling, the strengths in the marriage were almost completely overwhelmed.

Evaluation. Mr. and Mrs. G both subscribed to a very traditional value system. Mrs. G was a very nurturing person, who gained great self-worth from the successful rearing of her children. Although very bright, she had never worked, nor did she aspire to a career. Her husband was in concurrence with this arrangement, and had achieved professional and financial success, while his wife took care of home and hearth. The couple shared important mutual interests, a political outlook, and a highly satisfactory sexual life. These considerable strengths had usually overshadowed their inability to negotiate differences of opinion and interpretation.

Mr. G was accustomed to settling differences of opinion by demanding to get his own way. Mrs. G was entirely unable to confront her husband with her priorities. She either gave in, or made unilateral decisions and presented her husband with the accomplished fact, and waited to see how he would react. An early issue, raised at the first session, was a request for fee reduction, in spite of the fact that the couple was in a very comfortable financial situation. It appeared that Mr. G disapproved of her seeking counseling and considered it a waste of money. She defied him in coming, but characteristically attempted to placate him and take the focus off of her priorities by seeking a fee reduction. It also seemed that money, for both of the partners, was equated with emotional power, and in her neediness, she wanted to be given supplies of nurturance without paying.

The death of their daughter had caused the first serious crack in their relationship. Internally, Mrs. G had made some changes in her feelings toward Mr. G. Due to his failure to be supportive, he was no longer perfect in her eyes. Her own sense of self-worth had been battered by her inability to halt the course of her daughter's disease. However, she was aware that her strengths in dealing with terminal illness were far greater than her husband's, and this knowledge challenged the traditional foundation of their relationship.

However, she did not make any changes in the way that she handled her feelings with her husband, nor did he. But because of the internal change in attitude, the number and severity of arguments between them had escalated. For the duration of the arguments, they usually did not speak and ceased social and sexual contact, thus effectively terminating the positive interactions in the relationship.

The death of her father had reactivated the powerful grief for her daughter that had never been fully resolved. This grief blinded Mrs. G to any other options but caring for her mother in her home. She was totally committed to this path, and unable to compromise in any way.

Treatment.   Since Mr. G initially refused to come for joint counseling, Mrs. G entered individual counseling that, first, revolved around grief work and then focused her style of problem resolution with her husband.

The first two issues raised concerned the reactivated grief for her daughter, which occurred at the death of her father. This reactivated grief was unexpected, and Mrs. G had a mixed reaction. She was angry at her renewed suffering, expressing the feeling that she had already "paid her dues." With some work, she was able to identify anger at herself because she did not believe that her daughter would die (on the contrary, she was expecting improvement), and because she had been unable to save her child. With the reframing of her hopefulness as an expression of her good parenting, which served a function not only for herself, but for her dying child and the rest of the family, she felt more comfortable with her feelings. She began to enjoy some of her memories. At the same time, she worked on the anger at herself for being unable to save her child. In depth and detail, her expectations of good parenting were explored. Gradually, she came to understand and interpret for herself how she translated the terminal illness of her child as a serious attack on the quality of her mothering.

Finally, we dealt with the trauma that she experienced due to control issues and her difficulties in dealing with anger and aggression, in any form. The lack of control that she experienced ate at the roots of her confidence in herself and in her most basic assumptions of her world. She expressed her fear and concern about this issue in many ways: she was angry at the medical establishment for taking control of her daughter's care, but also terrified that her poor decisions might have deprived her child of the care that would have saved her life, and she was angry at family members and friends for their anticipatory mourning, expressed in gratitude that the child was not suffering anymore. Most destructively, she was angry at her husband for the form that his mourning took and for his inability to help her with the agonizing feelings that she was experiencing. Buried very deep was the fear of her own decline and death.

Many sessions were spent helping Mrs. G to ventilate and explore her feelings. She benefited a great deal from being able to express herself in a nonjudgmental atmosphere—an opportunity that she felt she could not get elsewhere. Next, we were able to reframe the issues so that the levels of meaning and communication were available to her. For instance, friends were trying to offer comfort while they felt very uncomfortable—not only with her grief, but with their inability to help her by changing the root cause of her grief. Most importantly, they were uncomfortable because her experience reminded them that such a difficult life event could happen to them too. This insight freed Mrs. G to examine her own fears of death and dying. In particular, she shared her fear of treatment. This precipitated discussion of issues of aging in general, and retirement specifically.

TASK- AND ACTION-ORIENTED TECHNIQUES

Stage III of the model is a system for facilitating life-style changes and includes techniques to help clients explore options and develop role flexibility. As the clients share their past and present achievements through the life review process, ego strengths and positive self-image are released. The process is further fostered by the achievement, in therapy, of age-related tasks. But, basically, the concrete nature of this approach, which makes use of direct suggestion and generally results in tangible objects and/or activities, is very appealing and necessary to a client group that is suffering and coping with a large volume of losses. The core issue with this clientele is the replacement of loss. They require not only the internal experience of replacement, which is accomplished through the mourning process, but the external representation as well.

Clients who are dealing with gross role changes, such as those involved in the retirement process, often need an approach that emphasizes the task-centered method (e.g., a retiring executive of a corporation will need to explore style and role changes of a broad and deep nature). Those who do not have adequate age-appropriate interests and activities can be helped to develop a stepwise plan to begin to explore their new environment and plethora of time. Younger couples, for whom retirement has not yet arrived, but is on the horizon of the future, can also make double use of this approach: first, in exploring interests and activities that are future-oriented in overt preparation for retirement, and second, in the development of role flexibility, which serves well at this stage of life. The great efficacy for the younger couples is that these concrete explorations will be done within the framework of the emotional issues of marital intimacy and expectation issues.

In activating this approach, the agreement is made with the client that the primary responsibility for reaching the goal lies with the client and not the worker. In this manner, independence and a sense of mastery are promoted. Tasks are structured and timed so that they will be more likely to be accomplished in whole or in part. Family members are invited and encouraged to support these goals, directly and indirectly. The major role of the therapist involves the continual reframing and validation of the observed role shifts and personality changes, in order to develop and facilitate role flexibility. To illustrate, let us now return to the case of Mr. and Mrs. G.

Case Example

As the anger and anxiety that Mrs. G was experiencing abated, it became possible to explore with her other outlets and expressions of her mourning and of the person who she was now. With the encouragement of the therapist, Mrs. G joined a self-help group. This step had the initial result of reactivating her anger, as the group was not helpful to her in a direct manner. The group members related to her as her friends had done; i.e., they challenged her right to mourn. They wondered at the acuteness of her feelings in the context of the length of time that had elapsed and the nature of the loss. Most of the group members had lost a spouse, which they considered a more crucial loss than hers. She required several sessions to work through her anger at their "insensitivity," but the experience taught her to respect the individuality and egocentricity of the mourning process. This recognition enabled her to be more accepting of her husband's style of mourning. So strong had her reaction been, that at one point, she had even doubted that he mourned.

When her anger resolved, she was able to find comfort and self-worth in helping others with their mourning process. Additionally, she gained insight into personal goals and motivations. With new-found awareness of the self-worth that she gained from the nurturing role, she actually sought to learn from the therapist how to help her fellow mourners.

TERMINATION

The termination process reviews the tasks that have been accomplished during the course of therapy—as well as those that remain—by using the list of developmental tasks of the mature-stage marriage. This review allows clients to place their struggles within a wider perspective and to appreciate their universal qualities. The individual and marital strengths that have been identified are readily accessible for review, and their importance and usefulness are underscored. The technique of continued review and reprioritizing of goals is discussed. An examination of Mrs. G's termination process will provide clarification.

Case Example

As might be expected, Mrs. G had difficulty in terminating. She missed an occasional meeting, and with some anxiety said that she felt that she could not do any more work unless her husband would come into therapy. After a hiatus of four months, Mr. G agreed to come in for one meeting, which served as the termination meeting. This was a clear example of the invisible partnership that goes on between the marital partner who does not participate in meetings and the psychotherapeutic process.

Mr. G took over the role of summarizing the marital strengths. He stated that he had enjoyed being married. He felt that they had a good sex life, and that they had agreed on roles and tasks within the marital relationship (i.e., Mrs. G always put him first and did not question his decisions).

Next, he expressed his awareness of the changes that had taken place. He felt that his wife saw him differently now (he used the term "monster"), because he did not want his mother-in-law to live with them. He also stated that his wife saw him as "a spoiled brat." He made it very clear that he did not like the changes that had occurred.

Mrs. G, on the other hand, used her opportunity to express her priorities. The issue of his reaction to the death of the daughter was mentioned between them for the first time. Mrs. G also made the connection for her husband that taking care of her mother helped her to deal with the death of her child. Mr. G was very quiet, clearly an extremely powerful reaction, as his normal demeanor was quite verbal and articulate.

The therapist reframed these events within the context of the family life cycle. The death of their daughter was placed within the framework of the task of launching children. While she would have left home in the normal course of events, her death became particularly traumatic as their other children were leaving the family of origin. Furthermore, she was the only girl and the baby of the family, and the loss of a child is what is developmentally termed "out of sequence," and therefore more difficult to deal with.

Mrs. G's need to nuture her mother was reframed from the positive perspective that it was one of her great personal strengths and that Mr. G had always enjoyed her nurturing qualities. It was noted that he had successfully shared these qualities with their children.

Finally, the therapist ventured the opinion that Mr. G mourned for his daughter also, and used his uncharacteristic silence as evidence. The differences in styles and expressions of mourning were discussed and it was suggested that the couple had many things to discuss after the meeting was over.

The couple did not come back. However, Mrs. G called to report on progress. Mr. G quickly reorganized his defenses. He told his wife that the results of the meeting were good for him but he felt foolish and additionally objected to the financial outlay. The couple were doing much better. Mr. G had not only withdrawn his objections to his mother-in-law residing with them, but was participating in planning for her care. He shared his mourning openly once, and his wife was able to see that she preferred him to be strong. She called his grief "terrible to see." Mrs. G felt much better about her marriage, and once again was able to see its positive aspects. Both she and her husband began participating in the self-help mourning group.

UNIQUE ASPECTS OF THE MODEL: A RETURN TO THE PAST

The developmental marital counseling model departs from standard marital counseling paradigms based on systems theory, in two ways: in the return to an emphasis on the past and in the identification of the client. Recent trends have shifted the therapeutic emphasis from the exploration of past trauma in order to produce insight, which in its turn is expected to produce change in current behavior, to an emphasis on examining the behavior in the "here and now." This approach has facilitated the generalization of issues and allowed both clients and therapists to observe how dysfunctional behavior carries over from one relationship to another. Problems and goals are easily identifiable and relevant and an additional framework has been created within which to work. The strengths of this approach are undeniable, and the "here and now" is an integral part of the model. However, we have seen that as people move through the latter phases of the life cycle, they have a need to reorder, reevaluate, reprioritize, and reintegrate their life experiences. To achieve these goals, they return to the past. This focus on the past appears to occur quite naturally, without any psychotherapeutic intervention, and generally yields good results in the development of positive self-image and continued interest and involvement in the life process. Thus, the past cannot be ignored, even if one wished to do so.

WHO IS THE CLIENT?

A more difficult issue involves the identification of the client. Due to the needs, issues, and resistances unique to an aging clientele, this model diverges from the current trend of conjoint interviewing and may see either member of the couple individually or use marital counseling modalities (see p. 65) that have guarded credibility today. This may confuse the issue of who the client is.

The emergence of systems theory led to accepted models of marital and family counseling that required at least the marital partners participating together, as a unit, in the therapeutic process. For many reasons, the use of conjoint interviewing is not always possible or desirable. Marital counseling with older couples in the mature-stage marriage will, most often, occur within a framework that includes a long-standing relationship between the marital partners, or will incorporate a long-standing relationship in the past as a part of its history, for one or both of the partners. In these circumstances, by definition, the marital issues, both developmental and psychodynamic, will be complicated and difficult, due to the great number of variables in the composition of the system, the duration of the system, and the issues of aging. Very often, the request is for individual therapy. There is an unwillingness to challenge a very old system (in the case of the long-term marriage) or a very new system (in the new remarriage late in life). Also, it is not uncommon for one member of the couple to refuse to involve him or herself in the therapy process. When these difficulties, or any others, are encountered, it is essential to begin where the client is and maintain flexibility of technique and openness to any treatment avenues that present themselves, while preserving the understanding of the problem as marital, when appropriate.

James Framo (1982) postulates that marital therapy is in a transitional phase between the medical model, which focuses on illness and the neurotic features in the individual spouses, and the systems model, which examines the unity of the marital dyad, the interaction between partners, and the system of the marriage as a part of larger systems. Although he does not see couples individually, he maintains that it is just as important to know what goes on inside people as to know what goes on between them—that neither dimension can be reduced to the other and that both are important. He quotes Whitaker's statement that when you treat a couple, you have three patients—the husband, the wife, and the relationship—and that therapy may focus on any one of these three at any given time.

The disincentives of collaborative and concurrent therapy described on the following page are clear and undeniable. They are expensive in time and money—two commodities that can be in short supply with an older clientele. For these reasons, as well as others, conjoint therapy is the treatment of choice. When the couple agrees to come together, it affords the advantages of strengthening the marital boundary, avoids the difficult issues of confidentiality with unshared secrets, maintains the transference issues within the marital dyad, and preserves the clarity of the client-therapist relationship.

However, there are many situations in which other models are indicated. Most pedestrian, of course, is when the client refuses joint counseling, as is often the case with an older clientele. Other examples include the individual whose psychodynamic problems are the root cause of marital distress; joint interviewing that becomes so hostile and chaotic that there are destructive effects on the marital relationship; and the couple who act out a negative transference with the therapist.

Counseling spouses separately can provide opportunities to activate a positive transference, a truce on marital hostility while individual expression can take place, and can even provide modeling of separation-individuation. Separation also supplies the therapist with an experience of the clients in a relational system outside the marriage.

Edna Wasser (1966), writing about counseling for older couples, suggests that a variety of techniques be employed and that joint interviewing, focused on the couple's current interaction and their daily problems in adjusting to one another, be combined with the availability of the counselor to each marital partner, individually, if it becomes obvious that the lifelong problems of each are affecting the marriage adversely. Jay Haley (1973) reports that Milton Erickson sanctions meeting individually or with the couple, depending on the situation.

Flexibility does not end with the choice of a client and a treatment format, as changes may well be necessary during the course of treatment. It is not uncommon to begin with individual therapy, progress to concurrent marital therapy, thence to conjoint marital therapy, and finally, to be involved in family therapy interviews and intergenerational interviews with as many as four generations of the family participating.

Mental health professionals who work with an older clientele are generally agreed that the complexity of the problems indicate multiple interventions. Dr. Dan Blazer (1982) goes further and states that multiple interventions, if orchestrated effectively, have an even greater chance of success.

Bernard L. Greene, editor, in the *The Psychotherapies of Marital Disharmonies* (1965), provides a description of six major categories of marital therapy techniques:

> *Counseling*: an orientation stressing sociocultural forces and explicitly acknowledging the implications of the "here and now" situation.
>
> *Individual Psychotherapy*: which he refers to as classical psychoanalysis, but here will be used to refer to any one-on-one psychotherapeutic relationship.
>
> *Collaborative*: the marital partners are treated by different therapists, who communicate for the purpose of maintaining the marriage.

Concurrent: both spouses are treated individually but synchronously by the same therapist.

Conjoint: both partners are seen together in the same session by the same therapist.

Combined: a combination of—

1. individual, concurrent, and conjoint sessions in various purposeful combinations.
2. family therapy.
3. group psychotherapy.

Working with an older clientele presents unique challenges (described in detail in Chapter 11), among which are the scarcity of basic knowledge about psychotherapy with older persons and the high rate of biological, social, and psychological change that this segment of the population is undergoing. New ground is being broken and we have much to learn. Flexibility of technique and questioning of theoretical rubric is essential in the search for efficacy and relevance in treatment. Different treatment modalities and combinations of client-therapist interaction should be thought of as a continuum of therapeutic options and the greatest amount of flexibility and creative latitude should be utilized in choosing a treatment format.

The therapeutic techniques described by Greene (1965) were developed for a target clientele primarily consisting of couples and families in the childrearing years. To account for the wide flexibility in style and theory behind the techniques, he cites the great variation in marital patterns, therapeutic failures, clinical necessity, advancing knowledge, and the changing sociocultural scene. The 1960s represented a time when the institution of marriage seemed to be undergoing changes and stresses that might destroy it as a viable social institution. Today, we know that variation in marital patterns has been the salient consequence of modern social and psychological changes, but at the time, concern prompted enormous interest in the problems, and therefore the solutions, of the family and there was a resultant explosion in knowledge, as the helping professions struggled to buttress the "failing" family.

Today, it is the turn of the older members of the population and the mature family structure to undergo the powerful social and psychological imperatives that recently applied mainly to younger American families. As the helping professions shift their focus to a new, emerging area of practice, many options must be explored and tested. The evolution of the methodology of psychotherapy has historically been tied to sociocultural developments and began with the focus on the individual within the context of his family of origin, expressed through the medium of the one-to-one therapeutic relationship. Treatment failures resulted in focal shifts to include the relationship between husband and wife, as well as their individual personalities, and responsive therapy models were developed. Continued therapeutic impasse and the growth in knowledge led to the inclusion of children, other family members, and even at times, nonrelated important others and institutional representatives to comprise what is loosely termed family therapy, intergenerational therapy and network therapy. As we seek to expand our knowledge base, all avenues, old and new, must be open to possibility.

Finally, crucial to the definition of the client is the premise that while the model does not conform to the form and techniques of conjoint marital therapy, it does not diverge from the principles of systems theory. Regardless of what combination of individuals is present during the psychotherapy session, the therapeutic framework always postulates that the individual is a part of many systems, does not operate separately from the system or systems of which he or she is a member, and that significant information relative to the therapeutic process will enter the membership systems, and will be returned to the therapeutic relationship system. These membership systems are viewed as interlocking, and therefore information, consequences, and reverberations can be felt by a great number of interlocking systems and may return to the psychotherapeutic arena from diverse, and at times, quite unexpected, sources.

CONCLUSIONS

The term of marital balance refers to the conformation of the partners' needs and patterns of mutual fulfillment in order to maintain an equilibrium in gratification that is acceptable to both. And, ultimately, the model seeks to restore marital balance. Perhaps because of the pervasive nature of the changes and disruptions in roles and life-style during the latter stages of the aging process, the concept of marital balance, and the concomitant goal of creating or restoring equilibrium in a marriage, is not only applicable to aged, as well as to younger couples, but also essential.

Using a combination of approaches with maximum flexibility in theoretical framework and technique allows for the greatest number of ideas and techniques to be brought to bear in the resolution of the most complicated and difficult issues, even those of long standing.

The older client, and the problems that he or she confronts, requires the maximum effort from the helping professions, if they (and, in time, ourselves) are not to be left alone and defenseless, to confront some of the more difficult and painful problems life has to offer.

PART II

Using the Developmental
Marital Counseling Model

5

Elements in the Evaluation

In the developmental marital therapy model, the evaluation process is particularly broad and complicated, since it deals with older couples, whose personal and marital history cover a lengthy time span and involve many connecting systems. The marriage is viewed as the creative, caretaking link in a series of interlocking subsystems, which together create the extended family system. A visual representation is shown in Figure 1 (p. 18).

THE PROCESS OF THE EVALUATION

Because of the complicated nature of the evaluation, a longer time frame may be needed to complete the process and arrive at a final diagnosis and treatment plan. Two to four sessions would be appropriate. This rather lengthy process also incorporates beginning goals in the therapeutic process. It allows the therapist to make a positive and empathic connection with the clients and begins the process of building trust. History taking has proved to be a valuable experience in the therapeutic process. Most couples understand that history taking and discussion of their problems, interests, and concerns relate directly to their request for help. The experience is often relatively easy, pleasant, and useful for the clients.

As the process broadens in scope, other positive benefits result. Along with the communication of important information for the therapeutic process, it imparts a sense of positive participation in and identification with the counseling process itself. Clients are often aware of gaining a greater understanding of their relationship and feel some lifting of the sense of blame and guilt. There may be enough distance from the present pain for the couple to be some-what supportive of each other during the history-taking process, which facilitates and promotes interaction between the partners.

COMPONENTS IN THE EVALUATION

The process of evaluation geared to the developmental marital therapy model consists of descriptions of the following elements:

1. The presenting marital issues that precipitated the referral, from both members of the couple;
2. Other marital issues, as they see them;
3. A history of this marriage and any prior marriages, along with an assessment of success or failure;
4. The intrapsychic dynamics of the individual partners;
5. The family-of-origin systems from which the individual partners emerged and to which each partner still has significant connections;
6. The developmental tasks that are engaging the current supply of emotional energy of both partners, which will establish their individual developmental stage;
7. The impact of the individual developmental stage and task on the marital relationship;
8. An assessment of the developmental stage of this marriage through an understanding of the developmental tasks engaging the family;
9. The impact of the family developmental tasks on the marital relationship and on the individual partners within the marriage;
10. An assessment of the need for medical or psychological testing.

In each dimension, the current determinants of behavior must be related to past determinants, and ego strengths and weaknesses taken into account.

The concept of family role is useful in making the connection between the internal processes of personality and those of family participation. Each person integrates into multiple family roles and also extrafamilial roles. The same person may adapt more effectively in one role than in another. Different interpersonal situations will bring alternate aspects of the personality into effective action. In one role, serious personality weakness may be evoked with negative consequences but in another, the exposure of this weakness may be minimal, or even elicit considerable ego strength. In different roles, the solution to conflict, the anxiety experienced, the defenses used and the skills and ego strengths employed, will vary significantly.

Of special importance is the congruity, or lack of it, among personal and familial roles. Certain roles fit, while others clash. An example of role incongruity involves the functions of mother and career woman (Carter & McGoldrick, 1980). A common marital complaint occurs when the wife runs into problems fulfilling her own, and others', expectations of parenting and career. There are several problematic permutations in this situation. The husband may support the career goals, but be unhelpful with the parental demands. The family of origin, from either side, may be unsupportive of career goals for the wife, or the wife may be unable to mitigate perfectionistic expectations in either role. In effect, successful adaptation in one role may favor adaptation in another role, or the reverse. In many senses, the operations of the personality are dependent on the social situation. When the interpersonal environment is radically altered, the adaptive responses of the individual must also change. This is especially apt when evaluating older couples, as they begin the process of role and environmental changes required in the successful marital adaptations in the latter stages of the life cycle (Glick & Kessler, 1980).

Many elements in the evaluation are standard to any assessment process, but others require some elucidation of their function and use in the model. A diagrammatic representation of the evaluation is shown in Figure 2 (see p. 74).

Previous Marital History

Previous marital history provides an understanding of the problems that are current in this relationship. It can offer valuable clues to issues in the present relationship and to personal dynamics and functioning, especially when placed together with the marital history of the present marriage. As such, it deserves an early position in the evaluative process.

In addition, a previous marriage implies unique special issues and concerns. It will probably represent a sense of failure for the partner, thus making problems in the current marriage much more threatening. The previous marriage may intrude on the current relationship in other ways as well. The marital partners may be using previous failure as a weapon in the battle against each other, i.e., threats of divorce, or the ex-partner may even be an active agent in the marriage. Weddings of adult children, holidays, and other occa-

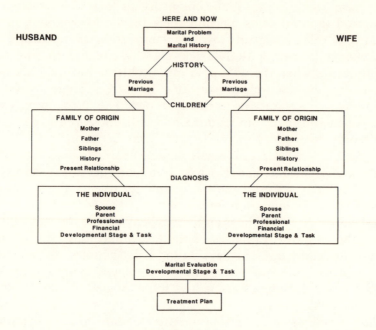

DIAGRAM OF THE ASSESSMENT

Figure 2

sions when families come together, for instance, can create dissension in a second relationship.

Family of Origin

Family-of-origin material is invaluable in gaining an understanding of present marital patterns and in assessing the individual dynamics of the partners. A major benefit in history taking is its potential facilitation of separation-individuation by the marriage partners (Fontane, 1979). The separation-individuation process is progressive, never fully completed, and provides ongoing opportunities for continued personal growth. It helps the clients see their parents as people, not just as parents, and themselves and their parents as separate human beings. Recognizing previous family patterns in one's own relationship renders that pattern amenable to change. The combination of being able to make sense out of what was confusing, along with having some hope in the ability to change expectations and behavior, helps a couple to feel better about themselves and to make progress toward more mature functioning.

This process is best accomplished when both members of the couple are present. This ensures that vital personal and family information is shared between the couple and allows the therapist to indicate the similarities or differences, and the connections between the histories of each partner. Thus, each partner is afforded possible new interpretations of his or her own and the partner's behavior and the process of modification of expectations and future behavior can begin.

The Individual History

Ultimately, any marital assessment tool seeks to evaluate the mental health of the relationship and the relation of the pathology of each partner to the disturbance of the relationship. As we have followed the individual through his or her family relationships, we have had an opportunity to gain a good understanding of how the individual has functioned in many roles and tasks in his or her relational life (Feldman, 1979). However, it is also important to obtain a sense of the personal, professional, and relational hopes and goals of the individual, separate from family task and role. The level of attainment of those goals and the sense of satisfaction with self, or lack of it, will have enormous impact on the marriage.

Furthermore, the marriage may be seen as enhancing personal and professional goals, or detracting from them; the personal goals of each partner may be at odds with each other as well. Past personal achievements and disappointments, goals, dreams, and future plans add the last essential ingredient in the equation that formulates the marital evaluation and the treatment plan.

Developmental Stage and Task

Interwoven with the individual, marital, and family histories is the assessment of the individual and family stage and task, which is done through reference to the developmental task and stage referred to in earlier chapters. It is important to note the developmental tasks at which the couple, as a partnership, succeeded and the individual developmental tasks in which each individual partner was successful. Examples would be a husband who was very successful at work, or a wife who had established many friends and contacts. These successful tasks will pinpoint areas of personal and marital strength that can be used later in the therapeutic process.

Case Example

The following is a case example illustrating the process and content of the evaluation using the developmental marital therapy model.

The Presenting Problem.   Mr. A called for marital counseling, citing financial problems of two years' duration. He gave his age as 68 and his wife's as 51. At the initial interview, they presented as an attractive, very well-dressed couple. Mrs. A appeared particularly youthful and good-looking, but despite their relatively large difference in age, the couple did not look incongruous together. The presenting problem was described as financial difficulties that had had a negative impact on the marriage. Five years previously, Mr. A had made heavy investments in the stock market. At one point, he was a paper millionaire and could look forward to a life of ease. Even so, his goal was not to retire, but to have the option to travel whenever he liked. His profession as a traveling salesman would have accommodated such a plan. However, this rosy prospect never materialized. Instead, Mr. A took a serious loss on his investment.

Very soon afterward, his earnings dropped dramatically due to the economic recession. Mrs. A attempted to help by starting a commission sales business in the same product line as her husband, which failed. The couple then made a geographical move in hopes of improving their earning potential. This strategy was also proving unsuccessful and the marital tension exploded in intensity. Mr. A felt that his wife ordered him around like an army officer while Mrs. A said that he had frequent temper outbursts and she felt verbally abused.

Description of Other Marital Issues.   The couple's financial "problems" were considerably complicated by the fact that neither was meeting his or her own expectations for achievement, either professionally or financially. They had considerable savings and other investments, but interest payments, and even some capital, were being used to meet current expenses, especially during particularly hard months. Mrs. A had had several jobs which had all proven unsatisfactory, and Mr. A had continued a traveling sales route with his customary product in an attempt to earn money. This was a bone of contention: Mrs. A maintained that he was not earning enough to cover the travel expenses. She wanted him to give up traveling sales and take a salaried job, which he refused to do. He felt that he had earned the money and had the right to decide how it would be spent. Mrs. A was very angry that the family financial resources were being used in this manner. She expressed concern that their resources would be depleted by the time she reached old age. Mr. A thought that she was overly pessimistic in her outlook and did not give him credit for caring about her when he was gone, nor for being able to plan for her future. Mr. A felt that his wife had lost respect for him, which she confirmed, adding, however, that he did not respect her either. She thought that he had supported her personal growth in the past, but now did not like the results.

In addition to this tense and strained environment, the couple reported that Mr. A had had very serious health problems in the last two years. He had had a bout with cancer and circulatory problems. The cancer treatment, though apparently successful, had resulted in a noticeable drop in physical capacity. He was no longer as active as he had been and appeared more forgetful than in times past.

At a very emotional meeting, Mrs. A expressed her inability to accept the possibility of retirement for her husband. She expressed very negative views on older people and a retired life-style, saying, "I'm not old and I'm not going to live like I am old." Mr. A expressed some sadness and anger that his wife would not allow him to even consider the possibility of retirement, but it was also clear that retirement was just as unacceptable to him.

Both members of the couple expressed strong and inflexible value systems. They made heavy use of projection and denial in defense of considerable internal vulnerability—attacks on self-esteem and anxiety related to the internal and external events that were negatively impacting the carefully built haven of their marriage, which both agreed had been excellent in the past.

Marital History. This was a second marriage for both partners and had been 18 years in duration. The As had met through mutual friends and both agreed that it was a passionate love match. Mr. A had three children from his previous marriage, two boys and a girl, and Mrs. A had two children from hers, a boy and a girl. They reported an excellent sexual relationship, appropriate intimacy in their personal relationship, and both had felt loved and respected. They were in remarkable agreement in describing the marriage, which seemed for both of them to be almost two marriages, the one before the financial problems and the one after the financial problems. In fact, their description of the first segment of their marriage had the quality of an extended honeymoon. Both traced the roots of the problems that they were experiencing currently back to those early days, but the roseate glow had then been strong enough to hold off a confrontation with the issues.

The early indications of later trouble showed up mainly in the parenting roles. Mr. A's children, in particular a daughter, were never integrated into the new family. The coldness remained to the present and his daughter still had little or no relationship with her father. Mrs. A's children also mirrored the potential weaknesses in the relationship. Her son became very attached to Mr. A and accepted him as a parent, but the daughter never established any connection with him and mourned her parents' divorce long past normal limits. Her relationship with Mrs. A remained conflicted also.

The good feelings that had characterized the early part of the relationship became nonexistent, or very rare, quite suddenly. The thin veneer of each partner's perfection in the eyes of the other was lost when Mr. A's invulnerable status was lost, both in his finances and his health and Mrs. A was unable to sustain and support any weakness in her husband. They became very competitive with each other, unable to provide any emotional support and comfort to each other in these difficult times, and totally involved in controlling each other. Neither showed capacity for introspection or insight at this time.

Previous Marital History.   Mr. A had married, at a young age, his childhood sweetheart, with the approval of his family. It was not a happy union. His first wife constantly nagged him to confront family members about business matters. He retaliated by staying away from home and when he was home, there was a great deal of arguing and shouting. His wife became hypochondriacal in retribution. He denied involvement with other women, or knowing his present wife, before the divorce.

Mr. A felt that his first wife had turned his children away from him. He did not consider that his own behavior toward his children or his subsequent interaction with his second family contributed to the present coldness and lack of relationship with his children.

Mrs. A also married young, in order to get away from home. She allowed her mother's approval of her first husband to sway her decision to marry this man. She claimed that she did not feel "love" for him. She cared for him, but was too immature to understand love. As she described this relationship, there was an overwhelming impression that she felt like a child, alone, and was trying to mimic a mature marital relationship. Her anxiety level was high, even discussing it years later.

Her first husband had difficulty supporting the family and the marriage was troubled with vague problems that drove Mrs. A to seek help. However, the couple did not benefit from marital counseling and the marriage dissolved when her husband confessed to some homosexual encounters.

Family-of-origin material was very colorful and nontraditional for both. Risk taking, adventure, and insecurity played a great part in both of the histories of the mothers of this couple.

Mr. A's Family of Origin. Mr. A's father, Alex, was 18 years older than his mother, Ann. He had immigrated to the United States in the late 1800s and established a family of three children, two boys and a girl. His first wife died in childbirth, and four years later, Alex married Ann, who was a distant relation through marriage. Ann's mother, after being widowed, had married a second time to Alex's father.

Ann had immigrated to America under very difficult circumstances. Since the whole family could not afford to come, Ann was chosen as the strongest and the most likely to succeed. She was sent under the protection of a family of fellow travelers, but the circumstances were so difficult that this plan soon broke down and Ann found herself alone at age 17, working, but having a difficult time surviving. Fortunately, she had contact with the extended family, and since Alex had lost his wife, the marriage was arranged as a good solution for both problems. Ann never learned to love her husband, although Alex apparently became fond of her. The couple fought a great deal and Ann was always cold to her husband. When they had a fight, Alex wrote letters to his wife. (This became a strategy that Mr. A later used in his own marriage.)

Ann did not want children, apparently because she already had three stepchildren, and had many abortions before becoming pregnant with Mr. A. She tried to abort him also, but the doctor refused, giving the reason that she had had too many abortions and another would endanger her health.

As children, Ann and Alex had been very poor, but by the time Ann married Alex, he had made a success of business and left a sizeable estate. The children were financially well cared for during their dependent years, and later worked for and inherited the business in nonequal shares. This legacy became a source of family disruption much later, in Mr. A's first marriage.

Mr. A never felt that he could please his mother. It seemed to him that she was never satisfied with any of his achievements and had never approved of him. She was still living, and this dynamic was still dominant in their relationship.

Alex died of a brain tumor when Mr. A was 16. He lovingly remembered his father as warm and affectionate.

Mrs. A's Family of Origin.   Mrs. A's parents were both American-born and shared a poverty-stricken background. It was an interfaith marriage. Her father, Ben, was Jewish, but her mother, Elaine, was not. Ben was one of 16 children. When he was young, his mother deserted several of the children. She sent the older ones, including Ben, out to live on their own, as she was no longer able to support them.

Elaine was deserted by a first husband, and Ben was her second marriage. At the time, it was quite a breach of convention for Ben to marry a non-Jewish woman, and especially, one who was divorced. Mrs. A described her mother as "a stunning woman"—very beautiful and smart, but passive. The marriage was conflicted and characterized by many arguments and criticism from Ben toward his wife. Mrs. A remembered asking her mother why she did not leave. Her mother replied that she had nowhere to go and no way to care for the children (Mrs. A and her sister). Mrs. A felt that Elaine never stood up to Ben and that she wanted peace at any price.

Mrs. A had a very poor relationship with her father. She stated that she had no feeling for him at all except dislike. She described him as a very insecure, unintelligent man who eked out a living. Ben was a "Jekyll and Hyde"; outside the home he was mild and polite, but at home he was a tyrant. Mrs. A said that he looked down on women. He was verbally abusive to Mrs. A, calling her a "jackass" and "stupid," and he would withhold her allowance over petty issues. Mrs. A's father favored her sister because the sister would sit on his lap and cater to him, but Mrs. A would not. The relationship between the two sisters was also poor, and has remained so. However, the sister also married very young to escape from the home. She met her husband in school when she was 13 and she later quit high school to marry him. Mrs. A said that the husband is wealthy and takes "good care of my sister."

The situation grew worse when Mrs. A was sexually abused as a child by a mentally ill teenage neighbor. Her parents apparently did not believe her and did not protect her from future assaults. Thus,

Mrs. A was left with no ways to validate herself, unprotected from sexual assault from the neighbor and verbal abuse from her father.

Diagnosis. Mrs. A presented herself as an ambitious woman with very high personal and professional goals. The yardstick by which she measured success was good looks and financial success. She had sustained a great deal of narcissistic injury in her family of origin, and subsequently in her first marriage. She had never felt adequately protected and cared for, with the exception of the first 10 years or so of the current marriage, when her narcissistic supplies and mirroring were good enough. At the present time, she was almost obsessed with the need to achieve and was angry that her husband had not achieved the goals she set for the couple. She was also angry that she still felt dependent and very connected to her husband.

Looking right and doing the right thing were extremely important to her as symbols of acceptance. She had a deficit in her ability to problem solve within relationships, and easily felt misunderstood and abused. She had little insight into the connection between the abuse that she suffered as a child and her tendency to feel abused in the present.

On the other hand, Mrs. A had considerable ego strengths. She was very good-looking and well groomed and projected an effective, yet feminine presence. She was bright, articulate, and able to form appropriate interpersonal relationships in most cases. It was mainly in the area of intimate personal relationships that she ran into difficulty. She performed well professionally and was very energetic and committed. Therefore, she was generally successful in her endeavors.

Her individual developmental stage was what Erikson (1950) described as generativity versus stagnation. She was actively engaged in reviewing life goals and making plans to achieve them.

Mr. A always felt a certain lack of acceptance in his family. His mother seemed to have had enough to do with her husband's children and apparently did not want her own. Thus, she was unable to give her son adequate and appropriate narcissistic supplies as a child. In this and other areas, the couple shared similar life experiences. This sense of incomplete family enfranchisement intensified when Mr. A received the smallest portion of the family business when his father died. The great age difference between him and his oldest brother ensured that he would retain the position of the "child" in the extended family network relational system. He had never been able to overcome his feelings that he was not accepted as an equal in the family. Indeed, he was not, and one reason was that his mother was still living, which reinforced his powerless position as the "son."

He had always defended against his feelings of insecurity and ineffectiveness with active projection, denial, and great attention to a successful facade. There was no question that his wife's facade was symbolic to him of his own successes.

Recent setbacks in health and professional standing had triggered the developmental tasks of late life, integrity versus despair. His displays of temper were a dysfunctional attempt to get more narcissistic supplies from his wife. He used denial to cope with the seriousness of his health and professional problems. His coping strategies added considerably to the problems. His goals and expectations in life were also very high and attached to concrete evidence of success, money, and consumer goods. Currently, he was displaying a very rigid and sparse range of coping devices and relational skills.

On the positive side, he also presented an intelligent, articulate, and effective presence. He was the consummate salesperson and his past and present successes, personally and professionally, were very easy to understand.

Developmentally, each member of this couple was coping with the tasks of different stages in the life cycle. Mrs. A was at the beginning of middle adulthood, involved in assessing goals and achievements and heading toward finalizing her life goals, with the object of maximizing her accomplishments in order to meet high personal ideals.

Triggered by the decline in his health, losses in family and friends, and the developments in his career, Mr. A was at the stage of late adulthood. These developments were forcing him to consider the possibility of a very unwelcome retirement, and perhaps the advent of dependency and death. He desperately needed his wife to support him in coping with his personal developmental tasks: accepting his life, being proud of his accomplishments and himself, winding down his active professional life, and preparing for the eventuality of death. Unfortunately, his request took the form of asking her to support his denial and projection. Mrs. A, involved in her own problems, was entirely unable to modify her own goals and was unresponsive to the possibility that she should modify her demands on him. She did experience feelings of guilt and concern about him, but these did not help mitigate her feelings of his and her own failure.

Their family histories indicated that neither of the partners had received empathic mirroring from parental figures and both had learned rigid and unyielding value systems and goals. Each had learned early a basic lack of trust in the opposite sex parent and they had both been taught to argue and demand, but not how to negotiate to get their needs met. They only knew how to break, not how to bend. Both would withdraw if their requests or demands were not met, only to explode in anger at a later time. The early years of the marriage had been so successful because there were no external stresses strong enough to impact negatively on their fragile system, and their need for positive mirroring was so strong that they could deny any but the most basic issues, which for them were money, success, and appearance. The couple had neither the inclination, the orientation, nor the energy to seek understanding and/or insight into their marital and personal problems.

Fortunately, the marriage had many strengths along with its weaknesses. The couple had done some successful parenting together. There was sincere caring, along with some healthy dependence on each other. They shared many values and goals and had a good social life. And most positive was their past history of marital, sexual, and personal success.

Treatment Plan. Marital therapy commenced with the goals of providing supportive therapy for the purpose of achieving an environment that might help them past this extremely painful crisis and, thus, leave them some energy to explore and gain insight into the psychodynamic and developmental issues which were impacting the marital bond.

In an initial treatment plan, the partners were seen individually for two successive weeks, and the third week, as a couple. The individual time allowed for:

1. Adequate ventilation of frustration in a nonthreatening atmosphere, which would help them to decrease their ventilation of anger and frustration on each other.
2. Personal mirroring, validation, and narcissistic supply as part of the therapeutic process, in order to mitigate the harsh demands and expectations that they had of each other.

The joint time was used:

1. To promote some relational skills between the partners.

2. To help them resolve some lesser issues.
3. To support the relationship ties.

CONCLUSIONS

Since it defines everything that follows it, the assessment phase is the single most crucial operation in the therapeutic process. Bloch and Simon (1982) have suggested that marital therapy has sometimes failed because of inadequate evaluation. A marital relationship has unique properties of its own, over and above the individual pathology of the partners. Conflict between marital partners is not simply an expression of the intrapsychic conflicts of each partner viewed in isolation. The marital relationship tends to influence and change each partner, and this in turn influences the relationship anew. Also, where there is marital conflict, it often involves prior conflicts between the respective partners and their families of origin. Nathan Ackerman wrote, in *The Psychotherapies of Marital Disharmony* (Greene, 1965), that the marital relationship neither exists nor evolves in isolation. It has a family in back of it and a family ahead of it.

Moreover, each partner is involved with personal developmental tasks, the outcome of which impacts on the self and on the marriage. The family, of which the marriage has been the creative link, is changing and evolving developmentally which, in turn, impacts on the individual partners and on the quality of the marital relationship.

6

Understanding and Using Developmental Theory in Marital Counseling with the Older Couple

Systems and change theories provide powerful frameworks for the organization of biological, psychological, and social events and the formulation of therapeutic models. Change occurs as a result of the process of dynamic interactions between individuals as they relate to their social, biological, and physical environments. The individual changes, as do the systems within which he or she operates, in an ongoing and indivisible process. When we view individuals as existing in relationship with other individuals, all of whom are in constant flux and operating within systems that are also undergoing a constant process of change, then the concept of developmental change and growth, both for individuals and systems, becomes not only possible, but necessary to understand human behavior.

The process of change has many properties. Change, in any social system, may occur in a random or planned manner. It may be gradual or rapid, horizontal or vertical, positive or negative, external or internal, and local or general in scope. Impact is greatest at the locus of change, and gradually grows weaker as the effects spread throughout the system. As the modification nears the system boundary, reaction occurs in a reverberating effect. In this fashion, one change produces another, theoretically to infinity. Indeed, human death may be viewed as occurring when no further change or adjustments can occur within the biological system as it exists. Any further change produces such drastic permutations that the organism no longer exists in its previously recognizable form.

DEVELOPMENTAL THEORY: THREE LIFE CYCLE THEORISTS

We are beginning to understand the naturally occurring phenomena that comprise the "aging" process, the environmental and physical factors that impact on the process and the effects of the aging process itself on the individual and the social structures of which he or she is a member. One theoretical framework that appears to offer very rich possibilities for interpreting and understanding the disparate biological, psychological, and social information we have about human beings and the human condition is the theory of aging referred to as life cycle theory or developmental theory. Within this framework, aging begins at birth and continues until death. The intervening time period is described as the span of human development.

This theory accounts for not only the demonstrable and regular changes in the individual which are perceptible throughout the life cycle, but also for the wide variations in aging that are observable from one individual to another. Furthermore, developmental theory dispenses with negative stereotyping in all age groups. The focus is on the tasks and capacities of human organisms and their attendant social structures at different stages of life. Emphasis is placed on the maximum realization of potential, rather than on deficits. And since biological markers of different stages of life are taken into account, we can incorporate the knowledge base from the chronological and disease models of aging, without ignoring the obvious differences in individuals of the same age group. Death is viewed as a limiting factor of life, which it is possible to transcend by building a future that we will not be here to see. Within this framework, the crisis is not the end of life, but how and where death will occur.

Finally, the concepts of developmental theory have removed any stigma from the idea of change. Change is not always welcome because it demands activity and effort. Yet, change is inherent in the definition of life. In the absence of change, there is an absence of life and we have come to understand that it is the rate and nature of change, and not change itself, that may produce negative outcome. In developmental theory, change is regarded as persistent and predictable and crisis is only one mechanism of change. Although the human system does not have limitless capacity to change, the continuous testing for the outer limits of adaptability is most likely the cutting edge of evolution and has undoubtedly led to the development of many current human capacities.

All developmental theorists share the following assumptions:

- Human beings continue to develop throughout life.
- Life unfolds in stages during the course of adulthood, as well as childhood.
- The stages are divided by transition periods that are sometimes punctuated with crises.
- Transitions provide opportunities for growth.
- Adulthood is to be examined in terms of the underlying health and strength people have to cope with change.

Erik Erikson (1950) described eight developmental stages in the life span: early childhood, childhood, latency, adolescence, early adulthood, mid-life transition, middle adulthood, and late adulthood. He conceived of the stages of development in terms of the life tasks to be accomplished during each stage and postulated that the inadequate completion of the tasks of one stage would make it difficult to succeed in the tasks of later stages. He described all of the stages in terms of the emotional consequences of the successful or unsuccessful negotiation, with stage-specific tasks. It is the final two stages of the life cycle, middle adulthood and late adulthood, which comprise the time span in the life cycle that is of specific interest for this book.

Developmental Tasks of Middle Adulthood

Middle adulthood is described in terms of generativity versus stagnation and begins at about age 50. The specific tasks described are to accept previous choices, to finalize goals, to prepare for a less work-oriented life, and finally, to retire. Clearly, the tasks are complicated and cover an enormous range of territory: from gearing up to reach the pinnacle of career to retirement.

Late adulthood begins at about age 70 and is described in terms of ego integrity versus despair. The tasks involved are the review of life decisions, the acceptance of life as it was and as it is, and the development of pride oneself and one's accomplishments in life—in essence, learning to give one's blessing to one's own life, and through that blessing, to be able to accept the inevitability of death.

George Vaillant (1977), on the other hand, views development through the maturation of ego defenses. This concept provides another dimension to developmental theory. Not only do individuals and tasks change and develop, but the mechanisms used to cope with life stage tasks also change and develop. He described a hierarchy of adaptive defense mechanisms, ranging from the primitive, such as denial, to the fully mature sublimation and repression. As he followed the subjects of his long-term research project, he was able to demonstrate conclusively that as they aged, even subjects who had been rated as poor on an emotional health scale used more mature adaptive defense mechanisms. And, importantly, he demonstrated how biological decrement may overwhelm mature adaptive mechanisms.

Vaillant conceptualized six life stages roughly corresponding to decades: identity formation, achievement of intimacy, career consolidation, generativity, keeping the meaning through passing the torch of culture, and the search for ego integrity. He is in basic agreement with the life stages described by Erikson, but he postulates that the isolated traumas of childhood are not as important to adjustment as the quality of sustained relationships and that women may mature differently from men, especially in the areas of career consolidation, attaining intimacy, and achieving generativity.

Daniel Levinson (1978) views developmental theory from a social systems perspective; he posits a life structure that has an internal and external aspect and is defined as the underlying pattern or design of a person's life. He divides the life span into four life stages, each about 25 years in length, during which there are long periods of stable structure building, followed by a transitional structure-changing period. The life stage tasks at this time are concerned with a reappraisal of the underlying life structure: exploring new possibilities; eliminating existing structures that no longer meet needs; changing structures, and working toward choices that provide a basis for new structure building. As entry into the new stage is consolidated, the tasks are structure building in nature. Crucial choices are made which create a structure and enrich it. And finally, the choice is made to pursue one's goals within the structure.

This transitional time span, during the entry from one period to another, reactivates the unresolved problems and deficits of previous periods. This concept seems particularly helpful in explaining how, in psychotherapy, pathology is observed that is obviously connected with an early stage of development, existing side by side with stunning achievement of the tasks of later stages of development. It may also explain how issues that have long been resolved might surface again quite suddenly. Levinson concurs with the need to do a study on women. With the exception of Bernice Neugarten's work (1964), which included subjects of both sexes, subsequent studies have had only male subjects.

Through all three of these concepts, we can follow a common thread with regard to task mastery. In a secure dependency environment, i.e, the family, the child develops self-respect and security progressively with the capacity for mastering the problems of his or her environment. As age advances into the last stage of life, there is declining power of mastery and, with it, declining security and self-respect. And adding to insecurity, the older person's declining powers of independent survival are not comparably associated with a supplementary secure dependency. It is this overlapping of the waning powers of maturity and the increasing helplessness of extreme old age that form the basis for the psychological picture that old age presents us, and triggers the crucial developmental task of maintaining ego integrity in the face of physical and mental decline.

Psychological Changes in Middle Adulthood

In order to make maximal use of the developmental perspective, it is necessary to explore the normal changes that occur during the process of growing older. The decade of 50 to 60 years of age represents an important turning point, with the restructuring of time and the formulation of new perceptions of self, time, and death. At no other time, with the exception of adolescence, does the biological component assume such a dominating role. Beginning with the climacteric, which announces the massive hormonal changes in the body, this period may last from 30 to 40 years and accounts for about one half of the adult life span. It is characterized by the gradual waning of physical capacities and the striking increment to the growth of wisdom and judgment in the individual. For example, intelligence scores at age 56 are significantly higher than at age 22.

As biological markers signal the changes occurring within the body, the perception of time shifts and the orientation of self begins to be measured in terms of the time remaining until one's death, rather than one's birth. In middle age, death becomes a real possibility for the self, and the change in the time perspective is intimately related to the personalization of death. This triggers an evaluation of self in terms of roles in life, satisfactions obtained, and goals for the future. There is a natural tendency to eliminate choices, as adjustment to the idea that time to reach goals and objectives is not infinite. Along with the elimination of choices, there is an apparent loss of willingness and ability to integrate wide ranges of stimuli, and the tolerance for change decreases. It is these changes that favor the ability to focus on depth and excellence.

It is precisely by the supplanting of sheer physical vigor with the development of mental powers, and by the creation and transmission of a social culture, that we show our uniquely human capacities. Physiology may inevitably suffer in the second half of life, but mental and social powers do not show a parallel decline. On the contrary, during the second half of life, human mental capacities can be most fully developed and used. Constitutional factors play a significant part in permitting a steady development of wisdom and know-how throughout life, but experiential and motivational forces are essential to the realization of this potential.

There is a good deal of evidence that the ability to interpret perceptions farsightedly, foresee complex consequences, and make wise decisions may be a function of a partnership of experience and intelligence. Furthermore, time and the maturation process are crucial in acquiring experience and developing intelligence. The executive processes, such as self-awareness, selectivity, and manipulation, assume central importance as a wide array of cognitive strategies are called into play to master the environment.

This period of time, which Erikson (1950) refers to as generativity versus stagnation, is potentially the peak productive period in human life. Socially, psychologically, and physically (in the absence of severe illness) the organism is poised for mental and professional achievement. The children have been raised and require much less physical energy; the mind is free to range over the increments of knowledge gained throughout life, and in general, adequate foundations have been laid which now allow for the building of new structures. The raging of hormones is quieter and sexuality assumes a secondary role in goal-directed activity. There is a heightened introspection in the mental life of the middle-aged person: stock taking, increased reflection, and above all, the structuring and restructuring of experience. This is the naturally occurring psychological event referred to as *reminiscence* in the middle-aged and is the precursor of the *life review process* in the elderly, which occurs further on in the continuum of psychological change as the organism proceeds through the aging process.

In summary, the major developmental tasks involved in middle age are learning to appreciate and make use of wisdom as opposed to relying upon physical prowess; socializing instead of sexualizing in relationships; developing the ability to shift emotional investment from one person to another and from one activity to another;

and finally, developing and deepening mental flexibility. Between the ages of 50 and 80, in relatively healthy individuals, age does not emerge as a major variable in the achievement and intention qualities of the personality; therefore, this period of explosive productivity may last for lengthy periods of time for many individuals. It is only when physical and/or mental health fail, that we see the changes more commonly associated with aging and old age in our society. Even then, if the decline is mainly physical in nature, the capacity to function professionally may be unaffected and even continue to grow and develop. Jay Haley discusses this paradox beautifully in his book, *Uncommon Therapy* (1973), when he talks about his mentor, Dr. Milton Erickson.

> Erickson has mastered an economy of therapeutic style, perhaps compensating for his physical weakness, which is like the strokes of a diamond cutter. He appears able to grasp the fundamentals of a human situation with remarkable quickness, and his therapeutic interventions are simple and precise, without wasted effort. With old age, his wisdom has increased, just at the time when he has lost the personal strength to put it into effect, which seems to be one of the inevitable ironies of life. (Epilogue)

Developmental Tasks of Late Adulthood

Cathetic flexibility (Neugarten, 1964), first identified as important in middle age, now requires new learning and redefinition, as for example, the relationship with adult children. *Mental flexibility*, which assumes increasing importance in middle age, also grows in significance.

Now, with advancing age, a whole new set of attributes are necessary for successful aging (Neugarten, 1970.) *Ego differentiation* and *ego transcendence* concern the emotional and social integrity of self. Ego differentiation is the capacity to pursue and enjoy a varied set of major activities in life and to value oneself for a number of personal attributes and roles. These abilities provide a sense of self-worth, enjoyment, and meaning in life. *Ego transcendence* is defined as the capacity to engage in a direct, active, emotionally gratifying manner with the people and events of daily life. It is also the ability to avoid preoccupation with private, self-centered desires, to show strong concern for others, and to find satisfaction in fulfilling the needs of others.

Other attributes assist in the achievement of the physical integrity of self. *Body transcendence* is the capacity to feel whole and worthwhile whether or not physical health is good and to avoid preoccupation with health and bodily comfort. This is increasingly important as health deteriorates. *Body satisfaction* is being satisfied with one's body in a way not directly related to health, vigor, or physical attractiveness. And, finally, *sexual integration* is the capacity to mesh one's sexual desires with other aspects of life.

Psychological Changes in Late Adulthood

One of the more noticeable psychological changes in late adulthood involves shifts in narcissistic investment and development. Normal narcissism revolves around the issues of self-worth, bodily integrity, and strength. Self-worth is defined as the ability to see oneself as loveable, special, altruistic, competent, responsible, and independent in the circumstances of one's life. With the advent of the sixth decade, physical changes begin to be more apparent, although still not impacting on the executive abilities to any great extent. However, along with the physical markers of decline, other narcissistic trauma are experienced such as retirement, separation from family and friends, financial problems, and finally, illness and death. Traumatic events increase in number and rate, and the individual becomes narcissistically vulnerable. One effect is that older people often become mildly depressive in reaction to losses and, feeling more and more isolated, turn in on themselves.

As the biological aging processes progress, the body signals more changes and decrements. A return to interest in the body is a normal response to negative changes in functioning and the wish to control and/or halt these changes. However, in exaggerated form, it can represent a decreased ability to repress and regulate primitive instinctive drives. The maturation of the personality is to some extent, a function of the regulation and repression of primitive instinctual tendencies. Major among these is sexual drive and the infantile interest in the body and its functions and many disease states common to older people, such as Parkinson's Disease, impair the ability to repress instinctual drives.

A dulling of recent memory can be observed, which may be attributable to mild trauma to the brain or to the emotional reaction of turning away from the painfulness of the present, or both. Older people find the possibility of mental decline very frightening. It is important to note that in most cases, mild memory loss is not the signal for more serious decline. However, significant organic problems may develop, such as Alzheimer's Disease or atherosclerotic disease, which accounts for severe memory loss or debility of mental functioning. However, it has been well documented that people with balanced personalities are able to withstand and compensate for considerable cerebral damage, while less balanced personalities may produce frank psychosis with a minimum of cerebral pathology. A striking phenomenon in old age is the intrinsic relationship between emotional problems and actual organic disease. These factors alone are a potent argument favoring the need for psychotherapy for older and elderly persons.

William Sze, in his book *The Human Life Cycle* (1975), illustrates the connection between emotional and organic disease when he discusses the ego adaptive mechanisms of older persons. He postulates that stress, i.e., the urgent pressure and severe strain produced either by inner conflicts or by the force of external circumstances, is the constant companion of the aged. He cites the signs of stress as *fear and anxiety*, which are reflected in generalized feelings of uncertainty; and *confusions and immobility*, which are reflected in the inability to plan and make decisions and in the *expression of hostility* (either explosive outbursts of anger or steady outpourings of resentment and frustration). The commonly used defenses that he cites parallel Vaillant's hierarchy of adaptive mechanisms. The more primitive defenses are *denial* of the disparity between the person's wish and reality, *regression* into dependency (which can be severe even to the point of incontinence), *flight* (i.e., wandering or leaving inappropriately, to the point of eccentricity and reclusiveness).

The more adaptive defenses are manipulation, integration, and sublimation. Manipulation, generally viewed in a negative light, nonetheless is a relatively healthy defense, since it indicates that the person is still vitally involved with the world. The process of manipulation is widely used, possibly because it relieves anxiety about dependency and death, since it provides the illusion of the ability to control circumstances. The most successful defenses are *sublimation* and *integration*. Many aged individuals who have reached a high level of integrative adaptation not only accept their restrictions, but also sublimate their anxieties by reaching out to others with warmth and support. They often display a highly developed sense of humor, which further broadens their perspective.

Summary

Socially defined time is interwoven with the biological and chronological measurements of time.

Expectations regarding age-appropriate behavior form an elaborate and pervasive system of norms governing behavior and provide one of the basic guidelines for social interaction. For instance, these norms determine the ways in which different age groups relate to each other, and operate as a system of checks and balances on behavior. Each age group has recognized rights, duties, and responsibilities, and the internalization of age norms and age group identification are important dimensions of the social and cultural context in which the course of the individual life span is viewed (Neugarten & Datan, 1973).

People are aware not only of the biological, chronological, and social clocks that operate in the various areas of their lives, but also of their own timing, and readily describe themselves as early, late, or on time in relation to major life events. In addition, the timing of life events and the reactions and adaptations of individuals to life events that occur out of schedule, provide powerful clues to the adult personality (Neugarten, 1970).

DEVELOPMENTAL STAGES IN THE FAMILY

In addition to the normal developmental stages through which the individual proceeds in the course of a lifetime, the family or families of which he or she is a member also proceed through identifiable and expectable developmental stages. The family is the first and the most important social system in which the individual acquires membership. In its function as mediator between the society and the individual, the family is the most sensitive of social systems. It is, at one and the same time, a refuge from the competitive and dangerous world outside, and the template, crucible, and barometer of other social systems in the society. Thus, the roles of individuals of all generations in a family shift and change according to the changing values in the workplace, the community, and the society. Individuals, and the systems within which they live, experience these changes according to the rules governing systems and change theories. Furthermore, systems, as well as individuals, have been shown to experience predictable changes in role, function, and structure, commonly referred to as stages.

Family life cycle theory is a relatively new therapeutic framework. It was not until Michael Solomon (1973) and Elizabeth Carter and Monica McGoldrick (1980) conceptualized the normal developmental stages of the family that family life cycle theory was applied in the treatment of families.

Michael Solomon conceptualized the family stages in terms of the "tasks" with which the family is engaged. He theorized that the family must master the tasks of one developmental stage before it can go on to master the tasks of the next. Families that avoid resolution of an early task will demonstrate chronic difficulties in family interaction, whereas those who have performed their tasks adequately are likely to demonstrate acute, stage-specific difficulties. All families will experience some difficulty and pressure moving from one stage to another. Solomon considers the family life cycle schema valuable because it equips the therapist with a diagnostic notion of the predominant family conflict. He divides the family life cycle into five stages, which are detailed below.

Stage I: The Marriage

The earliest task for spouses is to relinquish the family of origin as the perceived source of primary gratification and invest in the marital relationship as the primary need-meeting and gratification relationship in their existence. The family of origin will still provide significant relationships for both marital partners and the continuation of relationships between the marital partners and their families of origin is important to the development of both of these family systems. At this stage of the family development, the construction and implementation of the basic male and female roles of the marital partners are established and are likely to last throughout the marriage.

Stage II: The Birth of the Children

The marital pair must further solidify and, in some measure, institutionalize their relationship together as husband and wife. At the same time, they begin to develop and design their new roles as father and mother. A major issue at this stage is the establishment of the balance between the marital and parental roles. The children born have a defined role and need to be included in the family system. The parents will have fantasy projections, i.e., preconceived notions of what the child will be like, which must be reconciled with the reality of the child. If the children have been used to enable the marriage to continue, severe marital difficulties will ensue as the children prepare to separate and individuate and, eventually, leave home.

Stage III: Individuation of Family Members

This stage spans the departure of the first child to school through the adolescence of the last child. The family must move from the gratification and need satisfaction requirements of the basically dependent preschool child to a different parenting pattern based on the quasi-dependent relationships forged by the child's beginning socialization experience. Parental expectations must allow for progressively independent functioning and must be syntonic with the child's expectations of himself. The strivings of the adolescent for independence are mirrored throughout all members of the family, and are probably interrelated with the generativity usually seen at this stage in the parental generation of the family. This is an excellent example of how the tasks of the different generations of the family may be synergistic.

Stage IV: The Actual Departure of the Children

The primary task, at this stage, is for the family of origin to relinquish the role of primary gratification to the young adult members of the family and to reestablish the marital dyad. The older couple must incorporate the roles of in-laws and grandparents, and begin to develop new interests and hobbies. With changes in life expectancy, it is important to note that the last two stages in the family life cycle may well span half of the married life of the couple.

Stage V: The Integration of Loss

In the last stage of the family life cycle, the losses in social, economic, and physical functioning that are experienced by either or both marital partners are the basic issues needing resolution. The psychosocial dynamics tend to follow traditional conceptualizations of the necessity to grieve over loss, real or fantasied, before investment in future functioning is possible. Where the marriage has not been stabilized and the adult children not adequately individuated, there is the possibility of projection of the normal conflicts of this stage of the family life cycle onto the extended family. This eventuality can cause serious difficulties in continued family development for a large number of people.

Carter and McGoldrick (1980) conceptualized six stages in the family life cycle that are similar in many ways to earlier concepts, but they also take into account recent changes in the contemporary family. They have added a stage which shows the individual between families (the unattached young adult), have discussed the family position of the individual who never marries, and have added developmental stages in family breakup.

Carter and McGoldrick conceive of the family stages in terms of the major points at which family members enter and exit, thereby upsetting family homeostasis. It is their view that the central, underlying process to be negotiated is the expansion, contraction, and realignment of the relationship system to support the entry, exits, and development of family members in a functional way. They suggest that the emotional processes be viewed as "attitudes" and the "tasks" be viewed as relational status change. Thus, through separation of the content and process of the "task," they have refined the diagnostic criteria for therapeutic intervention.

SPECIAL ISSUES IN FAMILY DEVELOPMENTAL STAGE THEORY

Carter and McGoldrick (1980) discuss individuals who do not follow the norm in development—that is, the person who does not marry, or who marries but does not have children. They make the well-considered point that single and nonparental individuals go through the same stages as the standard population, since they must still relate to a family constellation and social network on the same issues that other families encounter: "One still lives within the context of those who went before him, those who go along with him, and those who will come after him."

In certain respects, those not following the norm have unique difficulties in shifting their status within their families. For example, the unmarried daughter, or the daughter without children, may be expected by other family members to care for elderly, dependent parents, without regard to other demands on time and energy or personal preference. Both sexes may have problems defining identity in relation to the family, given their expectations of his or her unmarried or childless status. The following case example illustrates some of these issues.

Case Example

Sylvia, a 70-year-old woman, requested counseling to discuss life-long problems with her 90-year-old mother. Sylvia was married but had no children and had recently retired from a very responsible position with the government. She always felt like a child in the presence of her mother, whom she could neither please nor satisfy. Furthermore, she was unable to assert her own needs and priorities when faced with those of her mother.

In many ways, Sylvia fit the changing profile of older Americans that has been described in Chapter 1. She had a doctorate in physical science, was financially well off, and in excellent health. She was unusual for her generation in that she had no children by choice. The precipitating factor that brought Sylvia for counseling was a scheduled visit with her mother. She was quite convinced that her retirement would be a signal to her mother that she was completely available to be at her mother's beck and call and was anticipating a host of demands that she felt unable and unwilling to meet. For years, these issues had been under control and had not assumed an important part in the relationship between mother and daughter. Now, ambivalence about retirement and her fears about physical decline and death for herself and her husband, intensified by real and imagined decline in her mother, combined to activate old issues and feelings of helplessness. She was very upset.

Short-term counseling gave Sylvia the opportunity to ventilate her feelings about retirement and her relationship with her mother. She gained insight into the role of her profession as an acceptable reason to distance herself from her mother and find acceptance for her own needs. With this insight, she was able to make the connection between her own retirement and the reactivation of the dependency issues which had always been an element in her relationship with her mother.

The therapist provided information on the normal processes and issues in aging, what she could expect, and what symptoms to look for that would herald negative changes in functioning so that she could make informed judgments about when her mother would require more care. This cognitive data enabled Sylvia to activate her excellent intellectual abilities.

She made the visit to her mother and reported back that the visit had gone very well, and furthermore, she had even been able to share with her mother some of her insecurities and feelings about retirement.

DEVELOPMENTAL STAGES IN FAMILY BREAKUP

Carter and McGoldrick (1980) have extended their ideas to include the additional phases required for families going through divorce and remarriage. Older couples still have a lower divorce rate than the population at large, but divorce is growing more prevalent and is therefore germane to marital counseling with an older population. The process begins with the decision to divorce. Developmental tasks include the acceptance of the inability to resolve the marital tensions sufficiently to continue the relationship and the crucial step of acceptance of one's own part in the failure of the marriage. Without the acceptance of individual responsibility, the necessary emotional separation cannot occur, even if a legal divorce takes place.

In the next stage, the breakup of the system is planned. Certain concrete issues must be concluded in order to complete the task of physically separating the family. The extended family network must be informed of the impending separation, and a beginning resolution of the issues of custody, maintenance payments, visitation, division of assets, and so forth takes place.

Next, the separation occurs and the mourning for the intact relationship begins in earnest. It is necessary to restructure marital and parental relationships and to realign relationships with the extended family. The boundary and the rules of the system are changed during this period.

The divorce is the formal ceremony which dissolves the relationship. The work of emotional divorce continues through overcoming hurt, anger, guilt, and so on. Fantasies of reunion are given up and the retrieval of hopes, dreams, and expectations of the marriage must occur. The post-divorce family has the basic task of keeping boundaries flexible enough to allow for continued, viable, and positive contact between both parents and the children, minor or adult.

Last, a three-stage developmental outline for the remarried family formation is described. First, there is entrance into the new relationship. With recovery from the loss of the first marriage comes a commitment to the concept of marriage, and the readiness to consider the formation of a new family and to deal with complexity and ambiguity.

Next, a new marriage and creation of a new family are planned. Accepting one's own fears and those of the new spouse and the children of both spouses about remarriage and forming a stepfamily is the first requirement. All members of the new stepfamily need time and patience to adjust to the complexity and ambiguity of multiple new roles and boundaries regarding space, time, membership, and authority, as well as dealing with the affective issues of guilt, loyalty, conflicts, unresolvable past hurts and so forth.

After the remarriage and the reconstitution of the family, family boundaries are restructured to allow for the inclusion of the new spouse as a stepparent. The realignment of relationships throughout the intertwining subsystems is necessary to make room for the relationships of all the children with biological parents, grandparents, and other extended family. The result is a very different family system, with much more permeable boundaries than are the rule for "intact" families.

DEVELOPMENTAL STAGES IN FAMILY BREAKUP: DEATH

For the older couple, the marriage most often ends due to death of a spouse. Therefore, for the purposes of our developmental marital therapy model, it is necessary to conceptualize the developmental stages that occur when the marriage is dissolved due to death. Since the children of older couples are most often adults settled in nuclear families of their own, the reconstituted family is likely to be a "family of one." The word "family" naturally conjures up the image of several people living together in prescribed relationship to one another. How, then, can one person be a family? Yet, developments in the modern family make it essential that we understand that the older widow or widower is a separate subgroup in the family network system—that is, a "family of one."

As Americans stretch the limits of longevity, the phenomenon of widowhood has become common, and older people, particularly women, will have the experience of surviving their spouses by a lengthy period of time. It has become the rule that after being widowed, older Americans, while maintaining the position of representatives of their generation in the extended family, continue to maintain separate residences and life-styles. All indications suggest that surviving older widows and widowers have very definite and separate interests and goals, differentiated from the other subgroups in the family network system. While family members are important to their life-style, for the most part, members of the older generation neither depend on nor heavily participate in the family network system on a *daily* basis, and most seek to remarry.

However, even without remarriage, it is clear that widows and widowers set up separate residences, life-styles, interests, and habits. They vigorously declare and defend their separation-individuation from the family network system until physical or mental impairment impel closer ties to caretaking family members. Even when there is a need for the family to provide supportive service, usually the most appreciated intervention will be minimal, and one which will support the familiar, comfortable, and independent lifestyle for as long as possible.

The younger generations in the family network system also work to protect the boundaries of the older family because the caregiving generation needs to maintain mobility and independent decision-making power in order to take advantage of economic opportunities, and the youngest members of the family network system have extended needs for nurture while they complete the complex and lengthy educational process now often necessary to achieve economic independence and success.

The death of any family member is a traumatic event for all members of the family network system. In the older generation dyad, death is an expected event and the members of the family network system have important and prescribed roles.

The process begins with the death of a spouse. The surviving member of a couple is protected by shock from the more painful feelings of loss. The extended family is usually very involved at this time and the intensive interaction further helps to insulate the surviving spouse from too rapid and too severe an impact from the loss of the partner and the relationship. At the same time, the arrangement and attendance of funeral rites have special importance, as they formalize the loss of the loved one and place a beginning measure of reality on the death. Grief, during this stage, is acutely felt and expressed physically through tears, lack of appetite, sleeplessness, restlessness, and so forth.

Next comes a transition stage during which the surviving spouse moves from an acute grief reaction to the mourning process. Friends, family members, and other social support systems will gradually withdraw services, time, and attention. The surviving spouse now has the space and the solitude to confront the pain of the loss. This phase is dominated with feelings of sadness, deprivation, and anger. There is little effort to resume normal social interaction, and usually only the absolute necessities of survival receive attention.

As the surviving spouse accepts the reality of widowhood, he or she assumes many roles which were previously carried out by the deceased. As the process of mourning continues, the mourner gradually comes to accept that the spouse will not return and the relationship begins to enter the realm of memory. Positive memories of the deceased spouse and of the intact relationship begin to provide emotional support in the mourning process. Relationships within the family and social network systems begin to change, sometimes painfully as relationships are lost or altered negatively.

The final stage is the one-person family. The surviving spouse is now actively engaged in rebuilding a life-style for the "family of one." Responsibilities and tasks, formerly carried out by the deceased partner, are no longer taken over as routine, but viewed in an objective framework. The surviving spouse takes over those functions with which he or she feels comfortable and competent to assume. Resources within the family, friends, or the community are located to assume the other functions. The role realignment within the family and the social network is solidified and meaningful and pleasurable activities are resumed with the framework that now allows for new freedom of movement and commitment. Positive and appropriate memories of the spouse now dominate thoughts about the past and the relationship has receded further into the realm of memory. The deceased spouse and the marital relationship can now be evaluated for positive and negative aspects. Validation of the lost relationship can take place, which will allow the surviving spouse to invest emotionally in other relationships.

REMARRIAGE AMONG OLDER COUPLES

In a system so large and complicated with real and remembered relationships, obligations, coping styles, habits, and so on, difficulties may arise from almost any source. In addition to confronting the same problems that face any newly married couple, older couples also have the developmental problems associated with their age and stage of life.

The following case example illuminates some of the issues involved in recommitting to a second marriage late in life. This example is especially interesting because it describes a failed interim relationship which reactivated a mourning process in the client.

Case Example

Samantha, aged 66, sought counseling shortly after her second marriage. She had been a widow for six years and had been very lonely.

In the two years immediately prior to her remarriage, she had had an interim relationship with another man. She said that they enjoyed each other's company and had a good sexual relationship, but he was unwilling to get married. When a friend's son introduced her to George, a widower, she made the decision to marry without knowing him very well, after concluding that her ex-boyfriend would always be unavailable. She thought George was a "good person." However, she also felt that George had rushed her into the relationship.

The event that precipitated Samantha to seek counseling was the announcement of the impending marriage of her ex-boyfriend to a friend of hers. Samantha reported strong feelings of jealousy and anger that her friend got so easily what she never could. Furthermore, the news caused her to question her decision to marry George and brought marital conflicts into sharp focus. She reported that George was impotent, which she had not known before the marriage and that sexually he was naive and selfish. She described him as suspicious, clinging, tight with money, and set in his ways. She reported that he did not try to resolve disagreements but placated her with meaningless statements. She felt that his son's opinions were more important to George than hers were, even when they involved issues that only concerned the couple. On the other hand, she showed her commitment to the marriage and her awareness that part of the problem was hers by stating, "I know I need to be more charitable, but I am withdrawing."

In spite of her identification of marital problems, she made the decision to deal with her feelings about her ex-boyfriend before she tackled the issues between herself and George. She did express an intent to ask George to consult a doctor about his impotence.

After the initial interview, she called in great distress about the amount and nature of the material that she had disclosed. Her guilt feelings were so strong that they had reactivated strong residual guilt feelings about leaving her parents in Europe during World War II, where they subsequently died during the Holocaust. This client-therapist interchange is an example of what may happen if clients divulge more information than they are comfortable with giving. This can be a particular dilemma with older clientele, who on the one hand have some sense of urgency about settling their problems, but on the other hand have been socialized to be reticent about personal and family affairs. Samantha did not return to counseling for three years but she was able to get enough relief from the ventilation of her feelings to enable her to regard the therapeutic contact in a positive light and thus return at a later date.

Her second request for counseling was precipitated by the unexpected death of one of her two adult sons. As a secondary issue, she worked a great deal on the problems that she had confronted in completing the commitment to the remarriage. There were problems with George's adult children and her adult children, and the differences in life-style alluded to earlier in the narrative. She learned to confront George's son and, soon, she could report that her relationship with her stepson was quite good. She began to entertain him and his two children regularly. Her own surviving son was divorced, and she worked at maintaining a relationship with her ex-daughter-in-law, which allowed her to see her grandchildren regularly, and she actively worked on keeping ties with the family of her deceased son. Considering that she had lost most of her immediate family in the Holocuast, she tolerated these family shifts and losses very well.

At termination of therapy, she reported that she and George had a solid and positive relationship. The sexual issue was never raised again, but she obviously regarded him with affection and gratitude for the companionship, affection, and security that the relationship afforded her. She was provided for financially if George were to precede her in death, and he supported her aims of maintaining family ties. Lastly, they regularly traveled to visit her grandchildren. Samantha was confirmed and comfortable in her original assessment of George as "a nice man."

CONCLUSIONS

Just as the individual proceeds through stages of development, the social systems within which he or she operates have their own developmental imperatives. These stages consist of the predictable changes in role, structure, and function of the social system as the individual proceeds through time. There are normal times when individuals and systems are particularly vulnerable. When it is necessary to master new tasks and events (e.g., new job, new home, new school), lack of experience and knowledge predisposes the utilization of a trial-and-error method of mastery. The lack of comfort and the experience of failures activate fears and fantasies of loss of control. As individuals and systems gain familiarity and mastery with new tasks, the feeling of control reasserts itself.

The transition period between one stage of development and the next—and the life events that signal the change—is doubly precarious. By definition, transitional periods require evaluations and exits and entrances from one system to another, along with the need to master new tasks. Defenses are, of necessity, in a minimal state and therefore, the unsuccessful resolution of the tasks of any of the earlier stages of development will now make themselves felt doubly.

The necessary expansion or contraction of the system can produce great psychic pain in the individual and the family.

Thus, an understanding not only of the psychodynamic factors, but also of the sociodynamic and the developmental dynamics of the individual and the couple or family are essential for the construction of an effective marital therapy model, and more so for older couples who not only have their foundations in their marital history, but are a unique product of its process as well.

7

Remodeling Theory and Practice for Use with an Older Population: The Marital Life Review

Attitudes and values regarding the aging process have resulted in the distinct neglect of mental health issues and treatment among the elderly, including the effects of their problems on their adult children. It was only when adult children found themselves in ever deeper difficulty in providing care for elderly, dependent family members that some attention began to be focused on individuals in the latter stages of the life cycle. As efforts were directed toward enabling adult children to provide care for their aging parents, it became clear that these caregivers also face many issues that are related to the aging process. The caregiver is at the beginning of a process that his or her elderly relative has nearly completed. The autonomy of young adulthood and the responsibilities of middle age evolve slowly into the dependency of old age—an unwelcome fall from power dictated by physical, social, and economic limitations. Erik Erikson (1950) believed that biological decline triggers a crisis for the ego, which is met with life cycle strengths that are accrued from earlier successes with developmental tasks. In late life, the process through which these ego strengths are accessed is the life review (Butler, 1963). Butler conceived the life review as

> a naturally occurring, universal mental process characterized by the progressive return to consciousness of past experiences, and particu-

larly, the resurgence of unresolved conflicts; simultaneously, and normally, these revived experiences and conflicts can be surveyed and reintegrated. This process is prompted by the realization of approaching dissolution and death, and the inability to maintain one's sense of personal invulnerability. It is further shaped by contemporaneous experiences, and its nature and outcome are affected by the lifelong unfolding of character. (p. 66)

This landmark work helped conceptualize a process in aging that is positive and productive (in most cases), and it suggested that personality and adaptive changes take place even in the final years of life.

The life review process is related to thoughts of death. Thus, it not only occurs in older adults, but also in younger persons who face death from terminal illness. However the life review is more commonly observed in the aged because of the proximity of life's termination, and perhaps because time is available and the defense provided by work is gone. For the individual who is in middle age [as young as 35 or 45 years old, according to Levinson (1978), Neugarten, (1970) and others], the relation of the life review arises indirectly from thoughts of death, in the perception of "limited" time and the life goals that are unlikely to be accomplished. According to Butler (1963), the life review is a process associated with adjustment to and acceptance of aging. Past unresolved conflicts are evaluated in an effort to reintegrate them more successfully. The life review process that has been set in motion by looking forward to death potentially proceeds toward personality reorganization. The more intense the unresolved conflicts, the more work is accomplished in the direction of reintegration. The process is active, but proceeds slowly. It may be episodic or continuous and occurs in some form for almost all older people.

Alterations in defensive operation do occur and it seems likely that a majority of older adults experience a substantial reorganization of personality, which may help to account for the evolution of such qualities as wisdom and serenity so often seen in the elderly (Getzel, 1983). In its mild form, the life review is reflected in increased reminiscence, nostalgia, and moderate regret. As the past files by, it is observed and evaluated by the ego. Reconsideration of past experiences and their meanings occur, often with revised and expanded understanding, which give new and significant meaning to one's life. Environmental circumstances may enhance the possibility of a positive outcome to the life review process, but successful reorganization is largely the function of the personality.

Butler (1963) suggested that "the life review is not synonymous with, but includes reminiscence; it is not alone either the unbidden return of memories, or the purposive seeking of them, although both may occur" (p. 67). In younger individuals (40-50), the life review is apparently preceded by a preparatory process of reminiscence. Offer and Sabshin (1984) suggest that middle-aged men and women go through a process of life review that is triggered by their children's growing autonomy. It also seems likely that the decline of aging parents would have great impact. The example of biological or mental decline in aging parents generates the awareness of the frailty of life and the human condition. The subsequent life review is probably, to some extent, reciprocal and empathic with the life review of the parents and is a part of the search for the meaning of life.

Reminiscence has become a popular pastime and families gather old pictures and possessions and interview elderly relatives to build a family tree. This is a powerful method to confirm personal identity in our impersonal world. We are only beginning to understand the function, process, and content of memory sharing in the latter stages of the life cycle. We do know that reminiscence occurs within and between generations and that confirmation of an individual's memories requires horizontal and vertical affirmation. Recounting of memories by the elderly appears to be an attempt to extend the relationships with the listener beyond the lifetime of the old person. People of all ages review their past at different times; they look back to understand the forces and experiences that have shaped their lives. While it appears that life events such as marriage, death, retirement, etc., are triggers for reminiscence, reminiscing, either positive or negative, may come at any point in the life cycle and may be used for a variety of purposes: entertainment, self-esteem maintenance, crisis coping, problem solving, and education.

It is clear that the natural biological and social events of the life span trigger a natural psychological process whose specific function is to enable older people to reorient their goals and means of goal achievement and to face the spectre of death for our elderly family members and for ourselves. The connection between natural biological and social events and psychological process has for some time been explored, documented, and utilized therapeutically for the beginning years of the life cycle. We have been slow, and unfortunately, uninterested, in exploring and utilizing this connection for the last years of the life span. This has been the essential element lacking in our theoretical thinking regarding psychotherapy with older adults.

ADAPTING AND USING THE LIFE REVIEW IN MARITAL THERAPY

A basic approach used in individual, marital, family, and group therapy is insight-oriented therapy. The life review and the marital life review are the methods used in the developmental marital therapy model to access the conscious and unconscious material used in the insight-oriented psychotherapy process. A normal element of the life review is the recovery of memories and the upswelling of the unconscious into consciousness. This process is generally regarded as one of the basic elements of the curative process. In addition, reviewing one's life appears to be a general response to crises of various types, of which marital problems may be one instance. For most older couples with marital problems, life review and marital life review are probably already in process before therapy begins. Thus, we have at our disposal a normal psychological process with enormous potential to effect positive outcome of the marital therapy process and to facilitate personal growth and development at the same time.

The Marital Life Review

The marital life review cannot be separated from the life review, since the marital relationship was and is part of the life of the individual. Rather, the marital life review is an indispensable part of the life review process. The focusing of reminiscence and the life review process on the marital relationship is a simple, natural, and powerful tool in marital therapy with older couples. It accesses all the potential benefits of a positive life review process, and it "joins with" the individual and relational issues of the couple, rather than intruding a new and unfamiliar process. An immediate positive effect is that the reminiscence about early days, the achievements of the relationship, and past solutions to marital conflicts and problems can strengthen the marital bond while working our present problems.

For the past 20 years, the consistent trend of theoretical developments in psychotherapy has been toward an understanding of human behavior as related to, and inseparable from, the systems to which the individual belongs. Such theoretical perspectives mandate the exploration of the membership systems of the individual. The marital chronology was introduced by Virginia Satir in 1964 as a means of easing the threat and providing hope in the early stages of therapy. The chronology offers a useful conceptual framework for structuring interviews and for eliciting and cross-referencing information about the past. Subsequently, the taking of marital history has become commonplace. Murray Bowen (1978) introduced the "family of origin" concept in working with adults and he commonly works with a multigenerational view of the family. The three-to-four-generational model makes it possible to keep therapy relevant to the couple's presenting symptoms and, at the same time, to go beyond them to the underlying patterns of the multigenerational system.

Frank Bockus (1980) discussed the value of reminiscence in couples therapy. He identified:

1. *Cast of characters*. Reminiscence can be used to gather data about the marriage and the marriage of the parents and important others in the lives of the couple.
2. *Themes of interaction*. Reminiscence will produce data on major interactional patterns among the members of the family; it will indicate the dominant tone of the interaction model between opposite sex parent and adult child (i.e., enmeshment, etc.); it will reveal the presence of displacement (an interaction that appears to have no connection with the present situation); and it will provide data on the symbolic reenactment of relationship patterns from the family of origin.

Bockus facilitates reminiscence with what he refers to as "an excursion led by the therapist." He feels that each partner's relationship with each of his or her parents is another variable that can be investigated through an excursion into the past. Of particular importance are the various relationship phases that have transpired with each parent, the times of dependency and autonomy, the times of possible overinvolvement, and those of disengagement. The replication of past fields of interaction, especially the family of origin, can shed light on the way each partner has mastered the critical relationship tasks of being close, being separate, ending relationships, and entering relationships. This information is critical in helping older couples, who are in a natural phase of reworking separation-individuation and dependency issues that have been triggered by life cycle events, such as retirement or illness (see Figure 3).

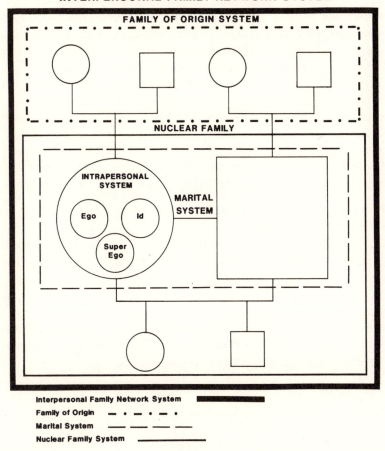

Figure 3

Eliciting the Life Review and the Marital Life Review

Michael Romaniuk reports in an unpublished paper that early cumulative research findings indicate that reminiscence is quite variable in "content, frequency, form, function, outcome, affect, and eliciting stimuli" (Getzel, 1983, p. 320). My own experience is that the process is so close to the surface and so natural that it is easily begun. An empathic question and a show of interest are often enough to keep a wealth of information flowing. However, other strategies are often helpful in both evoking material and classifying it for future use. Asking clients to write down memories and going over memorabilia with them are excellent activating mechanisms, but perhaps the best triggers are photographs. Muriel Reid (1985) feels that family photographs are mirrors which stimulate memories and can supply some surprising interpretations. Such factors as who appeared in pictures, where they are positioned in relation to each other, and so on, supply valuable information about family relationships, making a statement about what *is*, as well as what we would like the world to see about us. Pictures have many possible beneficial functions in the therapeutic process, but for purposes of the review process, whether it is individual or marital, they serve to validate the client's life, affirm growth, offer the possibility of reconnecting with previously held positive self-images, and correct memory distortions. The pictures that a client chooses to show the therapist also offer fertile ground for inquiry and interpretation.

Difficulties and Contraindications for the Life Review and the Marital Life Review

While beneficial in most cases, life review can reawaken painful and unresolved material that may have psychopathological manifestations. In severe form, the life review can result in anxiety, guilt, despair, and depression. Robert Butler (1963) believes that the more difficult and tragic manifestations may even be impossible to treat and that this situation contributes to the high suicide rate among the elderly. He identifies three types of individuals who appear to be especially prone to negative outcome:

1. People who always avoided the present and placed great emphasis on the future.
2. People who have consciously injured others.
3. People who are characterologically arrogant and prideful. (Their narcissism is disturbed by the realization of death's inevitability.)

Other circumstances exist which may make the life review unsuitable. When individuals avoid the present (or deny death) by retreating into the past, or when denial of age and the passage of time lead to inappropriate future-oriented behavior, the life review process may be counterproductive to therapeutic goals.

At times, even when the life review seems contraindicated, the marital life review can be evoked with good results. A major task in middle adulthood and late adulthood is the validation of self and personal achievements in life. When the life review process stimulates feelings of failure and lack of achievement, the marital life review may even serve as a substitute for the life review process, especially if the marriage has had specific positive aspects that can be evoked. It does this by focusing the client on a manageable entity that has positive aspects to support validation and self-worth. However, if there is evidence of undue anxiety or depression, efforts should be made to limit or stop the process. In the most severe instances, hospitalization or drug therapy may be required.

Marital life review is contraindicated when the process elicits generalized feelings of failure about the marriage, or when a negative outcome to the life review process has gotten projected onto the marriage. One function of the life review and the marital life review process is to facilitate acceptance of the aging process. If there is a negative outcome, the fear of aging may be overwhelming. Divorce may occur at this time, associated with the search for a younger mate in order to preserve the illusion of permanent youth or in response to the perception of personal or professional failure to achieve desired goals or ambitions. There may be a wish to discard everyone who was associated with past perceived failures.

The following case example illustrates how the negative outcome of the life review may be projected onto the marital relationship and destroy a previously successful marriage.

Case Example

The Presenting Problem. John and Jean had been married for 40 years and had four children. Jean requested counseling because her husband was threatening to leave the marriage.

History of the Problem. Marital problems had developed five years prior to application for counseling. After their last child graduated from high school and left home, John became deeply depressed for several months. Jean was aware of the depression, but felt powerless to help John. When he finally emerged from the depression, Jean reported, "It was as if I was married to a different person." Before the depression, John had been a caring and nurturing person, interested in Jean and her activities. Afterwards, he became angry, hostile, and abusive. He blamed her for his depression and began referring to Jean as "disgusting, stupid, fat, ugly, etc." He said that she was too incompetent to deal with any family business and had even suggested that a lawyer would "laugh at her" if she tried to get a divorce.

With the exception of sexual relations (which paradoxically remained good) and critical tirades, he terminated interaction with Jean. They rarely ate together, shared few activities, and never socialized together. John kept a bag packed and often threatened to leave for good. He claimed that as long as he had nothing to do with Jean and was disengaged from the relationship, he was very cheerful and happy. Jean attempted to cope with this behavior by ignoring it, waiting for it to pass, or by being cheerful, supportive, and nurturing. These responses only strengthened John's hostility. Finally, Jean began avoiding him and secretly drinking to calm herself. By the time she applied for counseling, Jean felt that she had reached the end of her rope and that divorce appeared imminent.

Marital History.   John and Jean met at a young age. Jean was 16 years old and described John as her first and only love. John also had limited experience with the opposite sex. They married while John was still in graduate school. He had been experiencing difficulty with school, and the decision to marry appeared to be influenced by this situation. He reported that he had never experienced any criticism or problems in an academic setting before, and he described his shock and fear that graduate school was so difficult. However, even though he discussed the two events in juxtaposition, he made no connection between the loneliness, fear, and need for emotional support aroused by his difficulties in graduate school and his decision to marry.

The couple began having children almost immediately and in spite of heavy family responsibilities, John was able to complete a doctorate in his field. The family had very little money or spare time, but did not feel deprived. They managed to do many things together and John took a very active interest in his children and his family. In fact, he appeared to take family responsibilities almost too seriously and often did not feel free to make choices that would have been more personally satisfying.

Theirs was a very traditional marriage. Jean did not work until the children were grown and John either made the decisions or had the final say in decision making. Both described their marriage as very good until John got depressed. Their sexual life had always been active and was appreciated by both. They were highly intelligent and shared many of the same interests, values, and activities.

John's Family of Origin.   John's family was financially stable and he thought that his parents were very happily married. They had one son and two daughters and John was the adored male heir. He tried very hard to please his parents and his sisters. The siblings got along well and, although not close, they had an ongoing relationship. The lack of closeness appeared to be due to distance and circumstance rather than any problems among the family members.

Both of John's parents were deceased. John did not speak much of his mother, but idolized his father, whom he saw as kind and wise. He was John's hero and role model. He offered the following story as an illustration of his father's character. When his father was very old and terminally ill, he was too weak to bathe. John's mother wanted to wash his feet so that he could be more comfortable. His father would not allow this, saying that he could not tolerate seeing his wife on her knees, at his feet. John cried when he told this story. He also commented that he did not want Jean at his feet either, but he did want to feel that the kind of devotion illustrated in this story existed in his marital relationship.

Jean's Family of Origin. Jean's parents were immigrants and financially insecure. They were not happily married and fought a great deal. Jean was the oldest of three children, a son and two daughters. She was her father's favorite and always felt that she was on exhibit. She was asked to play the piano, or demonstrate other achievements, for visitors and felt that she had to perform whether she wanted to or not. As she grew older, she felt required to perform in many areas in which she felt incompetent. For instance, she was pretty and popular, so her mother very strongly encouraged her to date, even boys much older than she. Jean felt very insecure dating, but her mother was so proud and so insistent that Jean felt that she had to comply.

The siblings did not get along very well and were competitive for parental attention. Jean's mother had died some years ago, but her father was still living. Jean and her brother were not speaking because her brother felt that Jean did not carry her share of caregiving for her father, even though Jean resided more than a thousand miles away and was employed full-time. Jean's sister did not speak to her father because of a misunderstanding about money. He had given one of her sister's children a large sum of money. The grandchild subsequently married without her grandfather's approval and there were very hard feelings between the generations.

Jean regarded her father as a very dependent personality who created a lot of unnecessary problems for all family members. She invited her father to visit her regularly, but often found these visits upsetting.

Individual Diagnosis. John was an intelligent individual with narcissistic and immature features to his personality. To ward off narcissistic insult, he devised a highly complicated and idealistic set of values and expectations for himself and others in which he was the final and only arbiter of standards and performance. These demands were focused on a highly individualistic value system that was loosely based on his idealistic concept of his father. He adopted extremely responsible attitudes that served to mask the reality that he was not functioning with a normative set of values and expectations. However, the discrepancy between his internal values and expectations and the demands of the external world provoked a good deal of anxiety that he kept under control by obsessive-compulsive attention to details.

Within this framework, he could deal with the narcissistic injuries that he first sustained in graduate school and later in his career. He also used investment in his family when he had to cope with criticism or failure. In the beginning, the marriage served to meet John's idealistic perception of the demands of his family of origin and allowed him to attain some badly needed feelings of success. It seemed clear that he needed emotional support and initially he found Jean's adoration and hero worship very soothing. He had no insight into his emotional needs and dependency issues, and regularly projected responsibility or blame for real or imagined failure onto family responsibilities and Jean's supposed incompetence. He was never able to meet his ego ideal of professional performance, and as time went on, the family also did not live up to his expectations. These shortcomings put pressure on his ability to validate himself in his role as a parent. With the children gone and retirement approaching, John began the process of reprioritization of goals and the life review. When he was unable to validate himself either professionally or personally, he went into a deep depression from which he was only able to emerge by a massive projection of blame and guilt onto his wife.

Jean had also been an adored child, and suffered her own narcissistic injuries, because she had never been allowed to fail. She escaped her role of extreme competence through marriage to John, where she was not only allowed to be incompetent, she was even expected to be so. Her discomfort with this role created only minimal problems, as her admiration for John was quite sincere and she was occupied with childrearing. She translated her interest in children into an education degree and when her children were in high school, she returned to teaching. Because Jean had not had the experience of trial and error in learning, and acceptance when she failed, she had an inordinate need for approval, which she equated with love. Jean had been taught to seek approval by entertaining people. Thus, she constantly used this approach with John. She could not tolerate conflict and had no idea of how to cope with arguments, which she always tried to smooth over. At times, her behavior was truly bizarre and provoked hostility and even tantrums from John.

Marital Diagnosis. This marriage had been successful for 35 years. The couple had had a positive personal and sexual relationship throughout that time. When John began his process of life review, which was triggered by a bout of illness and his impending retirement, he became deeply depressed. For him, the life review process was negative. He had delayed present gratification for future rewards, and now, he could not see the future. His individualistic value system and the refuge of the family as a place to succeed no longer served to protect him from the new narcissistic injuries of aging and eventual death. He found himself unable to validate his choices or his achievements. He emerged from the depression by galvanizing his anger and hostility around the marriage and Jean. He had always denied his dependency needs and now found himself in a trap: he felt that he could not stay in the marriage and he could not leave.

Jean, on the other hand, had spent her entire life deferring to others. She had a powerful need for approval and had developed few coping strategies to deal with conflict or anger, which she always internalized. She felt that it was so important to please others, that she was not aware of her own needs and wishes. The more hostile John became, the more Jean tried to defer to his opinions and wishes, and to entertain him in order to get approval. John became progressively angrier and more withdrawn. By the time that they came for counseling, this destructive cycle was well entrenched.

Treatment Plan. John was willing to come to counseling sessions only in order to provide information, or to help in his wife's counseling process. He was aware that he had major depressive episodes, but refused to seek treatment. He felt that he could deal with his problems on his own. He also agreed that there was hope for the marriage if Jean would get help. The therapist felt that John's defenses were so fragile, that the only workable plan would be one that allowed him to keep them in place. John and the therapist also agreed that if John showed symptoms of another major depression, he would discuss his symptoms with his family doctor and get medication, if indicated. John also made a contract stating that if he began having any suicidal thoughts, he would contact the therapist immediately. On this basis, it was agreed that he would come to sessions, as needed, for information or to further the therapeutic process for his wife.

The marital life review was evoked in order to provide information about John's view of the marital relationship, and also to connect him more strongly with the positive aspects in the marriage. The process appeared to be helpful and he agreed that he wanted to work on the marriage and would refrain from threatening to leave or leaving before discussing it with the therapist.

Jean entered counseling on a weekly basis. The goals were to work with her on "listening" to John, identifying her own feelings, and giving John some space and distance. To clarify, Jean was so intent on agreeing with John and avoiding conflict that she rarely heard what he was trying to say. Additionally, she was not in touch with her own feelings and wishes, and so she really was unable cogently to tell John what she wanted. Finally, although she did not realize it, Jean's need for approval and her constant attention-seeking behavior were quite smothering for John, who had reached the conclusion that Jean was unable to function without him, which caused him guilt about his wish to leave. While working with Jean on "listening" skills, the therapist encouraged her to get involved in activities on her own. She began to participate in a shell collecting club and a local dinner theater, which gave her an outlet for her acting talents and another place to get the approval she so desired. Jean began to take courses that would allow her to get a raise in salary, and also began to handle a lot of bureaucratic details that were necessary in running the house and their personal business. She also began to buy some household items that had been long overdue for purchase.

Concomitantly, she was encouraged to engage in her life review and marital life review. This process was very beneficial for Jean. She reaffirmed her choices and decisions, and in conjunction with her new recreational activities and responsibilities at home, she began to have a much more positive self-image. She began to feel competent to function on her own, should it become necessary. She also reached the conclusion that she wanted the marriage to work, if possible.

In joint meetings, she was helped to encourage John to get involved in his own activities, and even to leave home for short periods. John began to spend weekends away, and began to feel better about himself. His fear of dependency abated somewhat and he was able to admit that he had been frightened about going away since he did not know if he would be all right away from home. Once he saw that he could be away from Jean, John began to feel much more comfortable at home, and after some months of going to motels on the weekends, he discontinued the practice. It was also possible to do some work on communication during joint meetings. Both were able to do some exercises in "listening" (i.e., not interrupting, asking clarifying questions, and using the "I" message).

At the time that treatment was terminated, both Jean and John had a better sense of themselves as separate individuals. The relationship, though much smoother, was still fraught with very serious problems. John had not been entirely able to give up his projection of failure onto the marriage, and periodically felt very negative about the relationship. However, both had agreed to stay together and work at solutions.

CONCLUSIONS

The life review is a naturally occurring psychological phenomena that can be used and/or adapted, as in the marital life review, as an intrinsic part of the psychotherapeutic process. It is particularly useful in the process of marital counseling with older adults, since it is a potential source of positive feelings, is easily accessible and manageable, and supports the relationship through reminiscence of the good times with each other and the struggles overcome together.

8

Resolving Loss: Grief Therapy

Coping with loss is an integral part of the aging process in the latter stages of the life cycle. With increasing age, death begins to be a constant companion. Acquaintances, friends, and family members begin to die. Finally, it strikes at home with the death of one's spouses or one's own terminal illness. Moreover, death, final and devastating though it is, does not account for all of the losses experienced in late life. A great deal of psychological trauma seen in an older population is attributable to the object losses engendered in the cultural mores and expectations of personal performance, attributes, and achievements. Older individuals faced with the task of validating past choices, and the necessity for passing up new and exciting possibilities, experience a sense of irretrievable loss with the growing awareness that the organism is finite. Thus, mourning is a normal part of the developmental task of this stage of the life cycle. However, since mourning, at best, is discouraged in our society, the process is often covert and goes unrecognized. This secrecy may be one of the reasons that mourning in the elderly appears qualitatively different. Inhibition of overt grief is common, as is the channeling of grief into somatic reactions, both of which contribute to a prolonged and chronic grieving process.

In grief therapy, not only must we define loss and deal with the problems of number and rate of losses, but we must also examine the tools with which we cope with loss. Today, we see a resurgence of religious commitment in America. This trend may obscure the fact that among older people there has been a movement away from religion. The upsurge of technology in the first third of the century, along with the widespread political experimentation and unrest, spawned skepticism about religion. And while we are returning to religious commitment, the unquestioning belief in the dictates of church authority appears to be a thing of the past. The present group of older people who are facing the rigors of aging, decline, and eventual death will do so without the comforts of religion and the belief in an afterlife. For some, this absence provokes great fear, and the prospect of growing old and facing death may be difficult, or even intolerable.

The experience of loss and the subsequent mourning process have a heavy and potentially damaging impact on the mature-stage marriage. Possible effects include the following:

- The anger and depression that are normal components of the mourning process may be projected onto the spouse.
- Fear of one's own aging process may prompt the rejection of a long-term marriage, as an expression of the rejection of the aging process.
- Fear of the decline or death of the spouse may provoke a premature separation anxiety that can cripple longstanding, successful coping strategies.
- Differences in the expression of mourning may destroy positive feelings.

Other mourning reactions may impact on the marital relationship as well. Loss is always frightening, but it becomes destructive if the couple is being distanced, rather than drawn together, by the crisis of a loss.

DEFINITION OF LOSS

In recent times, our definition of what constitutes a *loss* has undergone major revision. In earlier eras, humans had little control over their destiny and, more important, they did not aspire to control. Much of their attention was focused on "life after death." Death was a familiar event throughout the life cycle of yesterday's family. Women often did not survive pregnancy and childbirth, so that step-families were fairly common and children were orphaned and on their own at a young age, especially among the poor. Furthermore, a large percentage of the population were recent immigrants. Families were broken apart, never to see or even hear from each other again. Other kinds of losses, such as jobs, physical attractiveness, and health, were accepted facts of life. While people grieved and mourned, the process appeared shorter and less painful than it is today or, as has been suggested in the literature, the distress caused by "loss" was consistently underestimated.

However, there were considerable mitigating circumstances that made the experience of loss and mourning significantly different from the experience today. People had few material goods to lose, much less expectation of economic achievement and stability, no prospect of control over the environment, and a cushion of religious belief. Moreover, the shared experience of frequent, regular losses and the sheer unremitting labor that was necessary for survival probably blunted the emotional agony of loss.

In the 1940s, mental health professionals began reporting that intense distress and emotional disturbance followed the experience of a loss (Bowlby, 1980). Although World War II was in progress and the population was experiencing great loss of life among young men, this phenomenon was concurrent with an observable rise in the standard of living and public health. The benefits of prosperity and health were quickly assimilated into the culture as expectations and our growing mastery of technology and medicine have fostered a denial fantasy that sees aging and death as curable. In our battle to dominate loss, we have shifted our attention to smaller and more controllable arenas, such as personal and material success. With this shift in emphasis, any change may be considered a *loss* and moreover, loss is considered controllable, and therefore, a personal failure. The ability to differentiate between losses may be impaired and the capacity to accept loss may be diminished.

In addition, bereavement has become unfashionable. Enormous stress is generated and great amounts of energy are expended in warding off loss and the resulting feeling of failure. Under these circumstances, when an unavoidable loss is finally confronted, the normal psychological mechanisms of mourning may even be aggravated—as opposed to times past when the normal mourning process seemed truncated and softened by circumstance.

SYMPTOMS OF GRIEF AND MOURNING

Grief

Bereavement after a death or a loss begins with a short period of shock, numbness and denial, followed by the symptoms of acute grief. Acute grief is characterized by somatic distress, which may manifest itself as tightness in the throat, shortness of breath, or almost any physical symptom. Crying is marked and only gradually decreases. Other possible characteristics of normal grief may be insomnia, vivid dreams, panic episodes, and disturbances of appetite and eating patterns (Blazer, 1982).

Along with physical distress, the mental state is altered. Feeling distant from people and from the environment is common and there is often intense pining for the absent person. These feelings are related to unconscious impulses to search for the lost object. At times, there are even misperceptions of the absent person's presence, almost auditory or visual hallucinations, which are extremely frightening.

Irritability, bitterness, and anger are characteristic of the mourning process, but are often surprising and disturbing to the bereaved, which causes additional distress (Bowlby, 1980). Events leading to the loss may be obsessively reviewed in a search for evidence of personal failure contributing to the loss of the object. This process appears to be associated with anger at the loss, and correlated with cultural expectations to control loss and the cultural view of loss as a personal failure.

Activity levels may fluctuate greatly, and the grief-stricken person may be unable to initiate or maintain organized patterns of behavior. He or she may become temporarily dependent on others to stimulate appropriate action. Even mundane tasks appear to require major expenditures of effort.

Mourning

Freud (1917/1961) noted that "reality testing has shown that the loved object no longer exists, and it proceeds to demand that all libido shall be withdrawn from its attachment to that object. This demand arouses considerable opposition. . ." (Bowlby, 1980, p. 65). Bowlby (1980) discusses the early phase of mourning in terms of the expression of angry strivings to recover the lost object and identifies these yearnings as a sign of health, enabling the mourner to relinquish the object in due time. There is general agreement among professionals who have worked with bereavement that this phase is quite painful. As behavioral disorganization and the permanence of loss are accepted, the result is despair. Only if old patterns of interaction are broken is it possible to develop new ones, related to new objects. Each time the individual is bereaved, he or she must accept the destruction of a part of his or her personality before reorganization toward a new object. This is a process that human beings are naturally reluctant to face.

Reproach is a natural feature of mourning and may be directed at the lost object, at the bereaved person him or herself, or toward others who may be seen as connected with the loss, such as doctors or supervisors. Reproach is also associated with attempts to recover the lost object and, in healthy mourning, positive memories of the lost person or object are strong enough to hold these angry reproaches in check, permitting limited expression and thus enabling the bereaved to master the loss.

Guilt plays a very important role in the mourning process and excessive guilt is often associated with a pathological mourning process. The circumstances of the death are often involved in the development of guilt as a part of mourning (for instance, if the bereaved persuaded a loved one to have a surgical procedure, or was merely in favor of the surgical procedure, that the loved one did not survive).

Case Example

The therapist first met the W couple at a workshop on aging. They were a striking couple: well dressed, good-looking, intelligent, and obviously prosperous. Mr. W was somewhat irritable and demanding. He was not entirely satisfied with the material presented, nor the answers to his questions. He appeared to be having a difficult time coping with retirement and wanted concrete answers to abstract questions. Mrs. W was much less critical and enjoyed the workshop not only for its intrinsic value, but as a worthwhile and interesting activity.

About a year later, Mrs. W contacted the therapist for counseling. Mr. W had died about a month previously. She was experiencing the acute phase of the grieving process and, in addition, was suffering from severe guilt feelings. She felt devastated and despairing. She described feeling totally disorganized and incapable of routine functioning. Her feelings of guilt focused on an argument that she and Mr. W. had had the day before he died, and the fact that she was not with him when he died.

Since retirement, the couple had been in disagreement about a variety of issues concerning a retired life-style. Mrs. W saw herself as an active person, who liked to participate in a variety of activities. Mr. W had an intellectual bent and most of all enjoyed sedentary and educational activities. He was happiest at home, but he often joined Mrs. W, albeit reluctantly. The argument the day before his death concerned a social engagement that she had forcefully insisted that he attend. She felt guilty because she had known that he had been ill for 15 years with all sorts of serious manifestations of cardiovascular disease. She felt that she should have understood that he probably did not want to go to the social function because he did not feel well. She was convinced that had she been more thoughtful and concerned about his health, he might be alive today. In addition, she felt guilty that she was not with him when he died. He had awakened early, at their vacation home. He kissed her and dressed quietly so as not to awaken her before he left for his daily walk. She was aware of his movements but said nothing, as she was still miffed due to the argument the day before. He was found later, dead, on the beach. Mrs. W was obsessed with concerns that he had been in pain or frightened before he died, and she had not been there to comfort him.

First, Mrs. W was allowed to ventilate her feelings and to cry. When the acute edge of her grief appeared somewhat blunted, the therapist began to wonder what it was like to know that one's husband was seriously ill for 15 years. This inquiry elicited a detailed description of the large number of health crises he had barely survived. Mrs. W also noted that Mr. W had retired early at the insistence of his doctor. Mr. W had been suffering life-threatening health crises since his middle 40s and, indeed, had died at the relatively young age of 61.

Mrs. W was encouraged to discuss her feelings about his health. She reported that her anxiety had reached such a peak that she had finally decided that life was impossible with "this sword hanging over my head." She made a conscious decision to give up worrying about his health, and to ignore his health problems when there were no symptoms or acute episodes that needed attention. While this decision had worked well for them, Mrs. W showed little insight into the benefits of this decision. It was only after many sessions, in which this topic was discussed from different perspectives, that Mrs. W could validate her decision as having allowed them to live as comfortably as they had, and could recognize the many wonderful and enjoyable experiences that they had shared, such as traveling together.

When she was able to accept the necessity of normality in their relationship (which included "normal" arguments and disagreements) as the exact quality that allowed them to have good times in their final years together, her guilt began to subside. She began to express normal regret at not being with him when he died and at having argued with him so soon before his death. No tempering of her regret was attempted. The possibility was accepted that he may have felt pain or fear as he was dying and that perhaps her presence would have helped him, but the possibility that he may have lost consciousness immediately and never known what happened was also raised. The therapist stressed that not knowing was difficult and that Mrs. W's wish to be with him when he died was a positive expression of all that was good in their relationship.

Pathological Mourning

Thus, the circumstances of the death can produce both normal and abnormal guilt Such behaviors on the part of the deceased as suicide, noncompliance with medical regimen, or persistence in seriously self-destructive habits, such as smoking or overeating, maximize angry feelings toward the deceased. Severe guilt may be felt if these angry feelings are directed back toward the self. The status of the relationship is also significant (i.e., a conflicted and ambivalent marital relationship is likely to result in abnormal guilt, springing from the knowledge, either conscious or unconscious, that the lost object was often wished dead).

A negative outcome of the mourning process is more likely when the bereaved have perceived their environment as blocking expression of such negative affects as guilt and anger. In a permissive, supportive environment where negative feelings can be aired, positive resolution of this crisis is generally reported (Grunebaum & Christ, 1976).

"One of the more pathological mourning styles is the denial of the reality of the loss. Instinctual response systems are not evoked to deal with the loss. The relationship with the lost person is continued in fantasy and because of the uncorrected reference to reality, the picture of the lost object becomes grossly distorted by idealization. The belief is kept secret in order to protect the fantasy. Another way that disorganization may be avoided is by the mechanism of ego-splitting, enabling the subject to contain completely self-contradictory beliefs about the reality of the loss. This type of mourning is rarely identified in research, but we can guess that these people are unwilling to participate in any discussion of their bereavement, for to do so would risk shattering their defense system" (Grunebaum & Christ, 1976, pp. 204–205). Yet, this type of bereavement may be more common than we realize. It would certainly be supported by the societal value system regarding "loss" and would account for the variety of grieving responses seen in psychotherapy (e.g., hasty remarriage, the incapacity for tolerating emotional pain resulting in delayed mourning, or substitution of grieving for seemingly insignificant objects). The end result of pathological mourning is the inability to connect again—and the capacity to engage in meaningful relationships is severely truncated.

The following case example illustrates the effects of a pathological mourning process that was provoked by the reactivation of earlier loss, and sustained through use of the immature defense mechanism of denial. The mourning process may be dramatically prolonged and complicated by the reactivation of earlier losses, especially when the earlier losses were unresolved or occurred at a young age. The result can be severe impairment of functioning at every level.

Case Example

Mrs. T was referred to the counselor by her daughter for an assessment. She was 66 years old, obese, and more or less functionally impaired in almost all the activities of daily living and in her social relationships. Her obesity was not a lifelong problem, but had emerged when her second husband died 20 years previously. Now it was a major health hazard and appeared to be a contributory factor in the impairment of her mental and physical functioning.

Mrs. T and her daughter reported Mrs T's history as follows. She was the youngest of three children. She had a brother seven years her senior, and a sister five years her senior. Their mother died when Mrs. T was nine years old and their father, who never remarried, raised the children with difficulty. The older sister, Celia, took on many functions of the absent mother. The family was very poor and all of the children had to work at young ages to help support the family. Mrs. T was sent to work at age 12, doing housework in exchange for room and board. One result of their poverty was that the children never finished high school, although education was an ideal valued by their father. It was clear that the family had been disrupted on many levels by the death of the mother. Although not members of the middle class, they had middle-class strivings, which became unreachable after the mother's death. She had contributed financially by keeping boarders, and this source of income was apparently crucial to the ability of the family to remain intact. Thus, at one stroke, the family lost a pivotal love object, parental figure, status and dreams, and valuable financial resources, which had a secondary result in the loss of educational and other concrete future opportunities for the surviving family members. The father's decision not to remarry rendered these losses permanent.

Another important factor in the family history was the family's involvement in the liberal politics of the day. As a consequence of this ideology, the father refused to accept charity during the Depression, preferring to go hungry. He felt that in the appopriate economic and political system, hungry people would be given food as their "right" and not as charity, which, to him suggested that they were unworthy or incapable of earning the food, rather than that the system was incapable of producing enough work. Mrs. T had a multitude of stories related to being hungry but she did not have insight into the connection between her physical hunger and her emotional hunger.

She married at age 18 and had one daughter after a very difficult pregnancy. She described her husband as very handsome, but irresponsible. He was unfaithful and had a serious gambling habit, leaving Mrs. T to support the family while he spent most of his money on extramarital affairs and gambling debts. Early in the marriage, Mrs. T renewed an old love affair, in self-defense, she felt. This relationship persisted for several years, but terminated when she divorced her first husband. Throughout the marriage, Mrs. T had worked in the retail clothing business. Untrained, she had returned to work out of necessity, to support the family. However, she did so well that the owners of the business had offered her a partnership.

Not long after the divorce, Mrs. T was introduced to her second husband, whom she married after a short courtship. This marriage lasted for ten years. She described Mr. T as the complete opposite in personality and character from the former men in her life. He was wealthy and extremely responsible, but had a very demanding and abrasive personality. Mrs. T constantly felt trapped and unhappy, but she also felt taken care of for the first time in her life.

Mr. T died when she was 47 years old. Initially, she was devastated, but after a very short time, she appeared to stop grieving. She returned to her home town and attempted to rekindle past relationships. This effort proved disappointing when old ties and life-styles were no longer attractive or acceptable to her. At this time, she began to exhibit some eccentricities. Her world began to focus on her house and her dog. She became obsessed with cleaning and decorating and refused to leave the dog. She completely rejected any attempts to enter a social system congruent with her time of life and her interests. Instead, she joined a young couples group and socialized within this circle. This move did produce some relationships of a parent-child nature, which were ongoing at present.

With time, her phobic reactions increased to serious proportions. She refused to leave the dog for any reason and exhibited increased unwillingness to leave the house. She developed fears about driving and she gained weight. She attempted to conceal these symptoms by claiming a lack of interest in social or family events that were not held in her house. She ignored any discussions or criticisms of her activities. Her family fostered her withdrawal by being overly critical on the one hand, while accepting her statements at face value on the other hand.

During this period of time, Mrs. T's daughter, Miriam, though she lived in a distant city and had family and professional obligations, began to notice these problems during visits. She expressed concern to her mother. With encouragement and support from her daughter, Mrs. T went into business. This venture proved to have both positive and negative effects. Mrs. T began to make some grossly inappropriate relationships with people she hired in her business. A progression of marginal and shady people began to populate Mrs. T's life. They began as employees, often paid well below standard wages, or even unpaid in a barter arrangement, i.e., work in exchange for items sold in the business. After establishing the initial relationships, Mrs. T inducted these people into the "family." She assigned them family names, such as "Aunt" or "Uncle," and delegated to them all sorts of personal and caretaking tasks, such as cooking for her. She required legitimate family members to accept them. She would even refuse to attend family gatherings if these people were not included. Furthermore, Mrs. T appeared not to notice the most bizarre behavior in her presence, i.e., a drunken faint, and increasingly used denial and fantasy to provide even a modicum of her needs.

At age 60, she had a health crisis that required the removal of half a lung. She retired after this surgery and since then had steadily deteriorated in function. At the time that she first sought counseling, she made no effort to take care of her personal hygiene. She was unkempt and often dirty, and allowed minor health problems, such as psoriasis, to go untreated. Her weight continued to climb, and she was beginning to suffer associated health problems. She stated that she was not lonely, could take care of herself, and enjoyed living alone. When confronted with any problems, such as her failure to pay bills, she laughed and said that sometimes she forgot, but claimed that she had lived in her community for 30 years and nobody would make trouble for her. She claimed that it was a mistake that her utilities had been turned off for nonpayment of bills.

Mrs. T had suffered early deprivation and had sustained multiple losses throughout her lifetime. In her younger years, her considerable intelligence and attractive personality enabled her to manage her dependency needs within acceptable limits. However, with the frequent losses in later life (known as "the insults of aging"), her inadequate and inappropriate defenses became more and more evident. Each loss provoked and sustained the primitive and regressed defense mechanisms that she used to cope with the early losses and deprivations in her life. Over time, her regression became pronounced as she continued to use denial and fantasy, almost to the point of psychosis. Currently, her regressive behavior was complicated by some mild mental impairment, probably the result of arteriosclerotic changes in the brain. The family was reluctant to place Mrs. T in a residential facility or a nursing home, and Mrs. T herself was very much opposed to leaving her home. It was decided to try psychotherapy in conjunction with some home health care to aid in the activities of daily living. The daughter took over payment of Mrs. T's bills.

Mrs. T tried psychotherapy for a few months, but was struck with a serious misfortune: her psychotherapist developed cancer and the relationship ended. Mrs. T did not return to psychotherapy and refused to try again. Within a short period of time, it became necessary to place Mrs. T in a board and care residential facility. After an initial adjustment period, Mrs. T was satisfied. Most of all, she enjoyed receiving care.

Identification

The final product of the mourning process is identification. Once again, there is controversy in determining whether the process of identification is considered normal (Bowlby, 1980). A cornerstone of psychoanalytical theory postulates that personality growth is dependent on the introjection of important aspects of objects that are lost or are in danger of being lost. The ego of the developing child thereafter is modified to conform to the introject. Developmental theory carries us a step further, showing that the human psyche continues to grow and change throughout the life cycle, and that the major catalysts for that growth and change are the connections and disconnections occurring steadily throughout life. Thus, in terms of bereavement, such an introjection, in the form of identification, serves the purpose of preserving, in memory, the relationship with the lost object, while allowing the disconnection of cathexis in preparation for new connections in the future.

Four possible forms of identification with the deceased have been described (Grunebaum & Christ, 1976). *Constructive identification* refers to identification with the vital, satisfying aspects of the object and the relationship. *Personality identification* refers to the adoption of mannerisms, traits, and characteristics of the loved one. These identifications are often transient and variable and their presence has a psychodynamic purpose. *Symptomatic identification* is strongly associated with pathological mourning and is expressed in what amounts to conversion symptoms. It represents the simultaneous unconscious gain of bringing back the lost object, as well as the punishment for abandonment. The maladaptive result is to allow the denial of the loss. *Depressive identification* is inevitable in mourning. When limited in extent, it is an accompaniment of healthy grief. However, in its pathological form, excessive and persistent, the mourner treats him or herself as the hated object, thus maintaining the fantasy that he or she has not lost it.

GRIEF AND MOURNING COUNSELING TECHNIQUES

Grief and mourning are observable phenomena. Freud (1917/1961) assumed that the process is natural and normal. He stated that, "Although grief involves grave departures from the normal attitude to life, it never occurs to us to regard it as a morbid condition and to hand the mourner over to medical treatment" (Grunebaum & Christ, 1976, p. 207). However, by 1961, Engel was arguing that it was valuable to regard grief as a disease syndrome in order to understand its mechanisms and its pathological forms. John Bowlby (1980), at the same time, propounded the view that the grief experience is inevitable, necessary, and growth promoting. This theory correlates with developmental theory and provides the basis for the inclusion of grief work in the developmental marital counseling model. With the social developments that have enlarged the number and categories of losses and the growth of the philosophy that loss is a personal failure, grief work is an essential component of counseling, especially with an older clientele.

To begin with, grief and mourning counseling techniques must take into account the needs expressed by the bereaved. Mourning individuals have reported that when they perceived the social environment as supportive, empathic, and encouraging of the expression of emotions, especially anger and guilt, they had a better health record and appeared to resolve their mourning in an uncomplicated manner (Bowlby, 1980). A group that had significant health deterioration in the year following bereavement reported a much higher rate of nonsupportive and restrictive modes of interpersonal interactions (Maddison, Viola & Walker, 1969). They perceived other people to be shocked by their feelings and reported expectations that they control the emotional manifestations of grief. People in their supportive network attempted to minimize feelings of grief by a process of generalization (i.e., pointing out the suffering of others and indicating how much grief it was appropriate to feel). Other nonsupportive examples were cited, such as individuals who were so inordinately upset that they appeared competitive, incongruously cheerful individuals, or those who claimed to share the grief and understand exactly how the bereaved are feeling (which is usually perceived as untrue). Other interactions that were reported to be unhelpful were attempts to focus on the present and the future (i.e., attempts to encourage interest in new activities and relationships or the resumption of old hobbies and occupations).

Interestingly, unsolicited discussions of religious topics were generally regarded as unhelpful. Subjects who held religious beliefs tended to regard such interventions as gratuitous and unnecessary, while subjects without any deep religious convictions found such attempts at comfort not only meaningless but extremely irritating.

The study concluded that the individuals' perceptions of their environment was variable (i.e., the bereaved person's longstanding mode of interpersonal relationship may contribute markedly to the perceived nonsupportiveness in the environment), and that the bereaved person's unrecognized hostile feelings could be projected onto the environment. However, the "objective" insensitivity, overt and covert hostility, failure of empathy, and relative or complete ignorance of the emotional needs of the bereaved individual played a much more significant role in poor outcome of the mourning process. Grunebaum and Christ (1976) felt that there was abundant evidence that many important individuals in the environment, including members of the helping professions, had behaved in ways that were in active opposition to those psychological processes required for the satisfactory resolution of object loss. Thus, we can see that the goal in grief work is not to hurry or end the mourning process nor to mitigate the emotional pain engendered by loss, but to encourage and support the accomplishment of a positive and uncomplicated mourning process.

We can identify three phases in the mourning process:

1. *Acute Phase.* This first phase is characterized by a high level of emotional and physical distress. Feelings of complete disorganization

and incapacity to function are normal. There is evidence that older people, especially the elderly, may get stuck in this phase of mourning. They exhibit a much higher level of physical problems than do their younger counterparts and they show decreased verbal expression of sadness and grief. This phenomenon was most clearly documented in a study of health records of London widows. Those over 65 showed an increased consultation rate for somatic symptoms, while those under 65 had increased consultation rates for psychological symptoms. In general, the acute phase may last up to a year, and may return cyclically for a longer period.

2. *Mid-Phase.* The mid-phase involves the exploration of the relationship with the lost object. The understanding of the role played by the lost object for the individual and in the mourner's past life cycle. This phase promotes the identification with the lost object, leading to the disconnection of the powerful emotional investment, and making way for new connections in the future.

3. *Reinvestment in New Relationships and Activities.* In this phase, the bereaved investigates him or herself after the loss: "Who am I now?" "What do I want to do?" "What can I do?" Positive and negative feelings about the new self are developed.

The entire cycle may be expected to last about five years. In the *acute phase* of mourning, there are four basic therapeutic tasks:

1. To provide support for the expression of both positive and negative feelings.
2. To shore up existing defenses.
3. To promote and assist in the construction of appropriate defenses.
4. To validate the pain of grief.

Central to the accomplishments of all the tasks in the mourning process is the establishment of a safe environment to express the feelings and behavior associated with grief. This is a time of regression which it is appropriate to support. Mourners may need assistance in accepting the idea that they cannot and do not want to function in many areas. Family cooperation should be sought until the mourner feels able to take on old and new tasks. The ventilation of all feelings, negative and positive, is encouraged. The source of the bereavement should be openly discussed and crying should not be discouraged unless the client appears uncomfortable. Among the elderly, it may be necessary to encourage and promote the expression of feelings verbally rather than physically. This approach can be complicated and difficult but it can be accomplished by continually referring back to the losses that are associated with the physical complaint. In so doing, one sensitizes clients to the connection between their physical complaints and their grief.

Rituals and ceremonies appropriate to the loss, such as memorial services, are to be encouraged. Finally, positive and negative feelings must be validated and the bereaved (and their support network) helped to understand that it is normal to feel unhappy and, perhaps most important, they do not have to like being unhappy.

The psychological work of mourning begins with shoring up of existing defenses and facilitating the development of mature and appropriate defense mechanisms. Defenses that appear negative and maladaptive in a younger person may allow the older person in a grief reaction to avoid dissolution of the personality, as the time of dependency and death approaches. Denial and projection are defenses that have been categorized by George Vaillant (1977) as primitive and possibly indicative of psychopathology. Yet denial and projection are sometimes useful and positive manifestations of coping with the harsher realities of life. Elisabeth Kubler-Ross (1969) has written about the adaptive features of denial during the process of coping with terminal illness.

Older people, however, do not need a diagnosis of terminal illness to force them to confront the advent of death; the mourning process described by Kubler-Ross is active to a greater or lesser extent in all older people. It begins with the psychological shift that orients the individual toward his or her death, and away from his or her birth. Therefore, all signs and symptoms that support the reality of the decline of the biological organism, as benign as gray hair or as serious as terminal illness, are subject to the acceptance process described by Kubler-Ross.

At times, the use of denial and/or projection may become excessive and counterproductive. Such extremes, of course, create difficult problems for families and other members in a support system. In such instances, the therapeutic goal is to assist in the mobilization of more appropriate use of denial and to teach, wherever possible, alternate defenses. The therapist can be helpful to the family, not as an interpreter of behavior, but through the use of careful reframing, in providing options for understanding the behavior of the "identified patient" or, if this is not possible, by underlining the positive aspects of the patient's behavior. As time cushions the shock of loss, denial can be supportively confronted.

The major task of the *mid-phase* is the in-depth exploration of the lost object and the mourner's relationship with the lost object. The strengths and weaknesses in the relationship are explored, along with the good times and the bad times and the arguments and angers. The needs that the deceased met and the roles that the deceased played (e.g., the family mediator, the favorite child), are important pieces of knowledge in the preparation for disengagement and reinvestment. The remaining fragments of the relationship are also explored (e.g., the child will always be the favorite child if he was before he died). It is in this operation that the life review comes into its own. At times, the two processes are so similar as to be indistinguishable, and mourning becomes an integral part of the life review process.

By mid-phase, mourners will be exhibiting their own natural coping styles that are based on the patterns used in the past to cope with other kinds of crises in their lives. For instance, a person engaged in the mourning process may sometimes limit the expression of his or her own grief and concentrate instead on aiding another bereaved individual, and thus, can project onto the other person his or her own feelings of grief, helplessness, yearning for the lost object, and anger at the desertion. This proxy response is, at times, not only a component of normal mourning (such as in joining a self-help mourning group), but may even be one of the tools used to begin to gain mastery over feelings of helplessness that enable the process of mourning to proceed. Identification with the lost object is encouraged.

In the *re-investment phase*, new roles, relationships, and views of self are tested. The client is encouraged to define verbally new roles for him or herself with friends, family, and work relationships. At times, it is difficult for old social systems to include clients in a new framework, without the lost object. This is a time when clients notice that they have lost friends who do not seem to know how to relate to them without their spouses. At times, it is the bereaved client who feels uncomfortable in some settings without the lost object. This can be a particularly difficult time for the client, understanding the indirect dimensions of his or her loss and beginning to rebuild a meaningful life-style. Within the framework of the marital counseling model described here, *termination* does not necessarily refer to termination of therapy, but to termination of grief counseling. There is a need to review the accomplishments of the grief counseling and the new insights, understandings, and roles accomplished. These then need to be fitted into the larger goals of the marital counseling.

Case Example

The following case study illustrates the effects on a stable marriage of the mourning process caused by retirement and ill health.

Mrs. C was a 72-year-old former teacher who had retired due to ill health two years prior to her request for marital counseling. During the intake process, Mrs. C stated that she had found her marriage increasingly unsatisfactory in the past two years and was seriously considering permanent separation. Divorce was not a viable option to her, as "it would violate all my principles and integrity, something I've not been forced to do in the past and will not consider at this stage of my life."

A marital history was obtained. The couple had a long-distance courtship, consisting mainly of correspondence, for a short time before marrying. Mrs. C felt that had she known her husband better, she would not have married him. The basic problems described concerned commitment and boundaries. Mrs. C questioned her husband's commitment to her and offered examples of his inability to stand up for her, especially in front of his mother. She felt that he had chosen loyalty to his mother over loyalty to her. She also stated that Mr. C never engaged with her emotionally and complained that she could never have an open, impassioned discussion with him. He would go away, either literally or figuratively.

Mr. C was in agreement with the major representations of the problems in their relationship. His interpretations of these representations differed significantly, however. The emotionality and passion that Mrs. C brought to discussions were viewed by Mr. C as coercion. Her need for companionship and interaction intruded on his inner life and his need to be alone and quiet. He felt that his politeness and duty to his mother had been misinterpreted by his wife as a defect in marital loyalty. At 75 years old, he was carrying on an active and successful one-man business. He was also considering separation in order to have "peace."

Both members of the couple were highly intelligent and accomplished, with an extremely strong sense of ethical and moral behavior. Both were exhausted with the issues and experienced a sense of depletion, helplessness, and hopelessness concerning the resolution of their problems.

Preliminary evaluation indicated that this was a late mature-stage marital relationship. Anxiety, generated by serious health decline and the possibility of death, as well as the disruption in life patterns occasioned by retirement, had reactivated a complex set of longstanding conflicts. These had remained quiescent with the aid of sublimation and the successful engagement with the marital tasks of earlier stages in the family life cycle. Because some marital conflicts had been sublimated in professional activities, Mrs. C had never seriously engaged in the preparatory tasks for retirement. Indeed, she appeared never to have even thought of the possibility of retiring. When faced with the reality of ill health and retirement, she suffered a regression in her defensive postures and began to use denial and projection with greater frequency and less satisfactory results. Mr. C, always unable to deal with his wife's strong emotions, was unable to help her cope with these intense feelings. Furthermore, her inability to work was a reminder that he would not be able to continue working indefinitely. This realization was particularly threatening to him, as he had always escaped the intensity of the relationship by withdrawing into work and his private internal space.

The couple was unable to validate other stages of their marriage and had lost most of their capacity to nurture each other. Mrs. C had lost her sense of meaning within the marriage, the extended family network system, and society. Both partners were unable to think in terms of goals. Rather, they attempted to distance themselves from the painful issues that battered them both, not the least of which was anxiety about the physical dependency and death that the future might bring.

A treatment plan was formulated for each member of the couple to enter individual counseling with separate therapists on a weekly basis and a monthly joint meeting to work on marital issues. This plan was based on Mrs. C's refusal to enter joint counseling with her husband. An earlier experience with marital counseling had been very negative for her and she had felt "blamed" for all the marital problems. Separate therapists were necessary due to the trust issues that were raised in the evaluation process and the sense that Mrs. C needed something of her own, both to enhance self-worth, and as an unstated message that she did have personal problems that intruded on the marriage. It was further agreed that during individual counseling, the goal for Mrs. C would be to work on shoring up her sense of self-worth and the goal for Mr. C would be to support him in confronting Mrs. C with his feelings. The psychotherapists cooperated in the regular exchange of material.

Mrs. C described a very passionate and joyous sex life, which had more or less ceased approximately 10 years ago, due to her loss of health. Mr. C cried when discussing this same issue. The couple had four highly intelligent and successful children and numerous grand-children. The extended family relationships were close, warm, and appropriate. Both were able to maintain close ties with grandchildren, even those who lived at a distance and were seen only occasionally. This was particularly true of Mrs. C, who also prided herself on being a good mother-in-law and made a point of not interfering in her children's marriages.

As the marital life review continued, Mrs. C described the financially difficult early years of the marriage, during the Depression, when jobs were difficult to find. She did not present this period as a problem, but merely described it. Despite their excellent sexual adjustment, Mrs. C was not happy and had already identified the issues previously stated as her presenting complaints. She went home for a visit, and was counseled by her father not to leave her husband. Mrs. C felt that his advice was poor; this was the one complaint that she voiced against her father. However, she followed his advice and found her gratification in companionship with her children and others and channeled her emotional intensity into intellectual pursuits.

Mr. C's passivity continued to be a problem in other areas. He had difficulty with jobs and it was Mrs. C who encouraged him to go into business for himself. She felt that he would not have done it if she had not pressured him, but she was able to view this interaction in a positive light. An ongoing source of distress to Mrs. C was the payment of the family bills. This was Mr. C's responsibility, at his insistence, and he was very lax in the discharge of his duties. On numerous occasions, Mrs. C had been embarrassed by his style of handling the family finances.

In spite of these problems, it was clear that the couple had worked out a modus vivendi. They were in substantial agreement concerning their professional and parental successes and both viewed these years as good years.

As the therapeutic process developed, enabling Mrs. C to repair her severely damaged self-image, she began to focus more intensely on her retirement. She identified the cause of her boredom in the lack of meaningful tasks and her enforced inactive life-style due to poor health. She gained insight into how she projected her anxiety about her health onto her husband and she began to realize how much she had hoped and expected that he would alleviate her boredom. This growth in understanding was a freeing process for her.

Subsequently, she began to activate her well-developed sense of community responsibility. With the help of her adult children, who researched volunteer projects, Mrs. C was soon involved in teaching again, this time on a level that did not endanger her health or tire her to the point where she was constantly reminded of her physical frailty. Another problem surfaced when it became clear that Mrs. C's use of denial in coping with her physical debility had led to inadequate medical attention. With Mrs. C's approval and cooperation, family members were recruited to participate in planning and monitoring Mrs. C's future health care plans.

On a parallel track, Mr. C was helped to understand that his withdrawal response, which was complementary and adaptive in many ways, at times only inflamed his wife. He spent a great deal of time looking at his characteristic patterns of relating to women. Apparently, he covered his deep feelings of resentment at what he considered controlling behavior with passive-aggressive responses, which he justified as gentlemanly behavior. He was less introspective than his wife, and much of the therapeutic work was supportive rather than insight-oriented. His positive role achievements as a father and a breadwinner were highlighted consistently, and both Mr. and Mrs. C were helped to identify their successes in the spousal role. Mr. C was supported to confront Mrs. C with his need for some quiet time alone at home, but also to plan for time to be with her. Mr. C did a lot of mourning for the physical and emotional losses that the relationship had sustained over the years. Mrs. C did more mourning for her personal losses.

At termination of therapy, Mrs. C could identify the ways in which retirement and ill health had negatively impacted on the marriage. She felt validated in her assessment that her husband had difficulty sustaining intimacy, but she had gained greater insight into the complementarity of the relationship. She had also experienced a very strong validating experience with her young adult grandchildren. This proved to be the pivotal point that allowed her to explore her role in the extended family network. Thus, she discovered that her ill health and retirement from professional life had not affected her central role in the extended family system. It was almost possible to see the depression begin to lift from her shoulders. Even her halting gait improved.

Mr. C, as might be expected, had less colorful and dramatic gains from his experience. As Mrs. C redirected her needs into different and wider channels, she withdrew much of the pressure and hostility from the relationship. Mr. C was then able to be somewhat more direct in his communication. He was intensely grateful and relieved that the situation had apparently resolved, and once again, they could enjoy and appreciate each other for their positive qualities. He receded quietly and smiling to the background.

Mrs. C, on the other hand, terminated therapy with the light of battle in her eye. She realized that the passion that she brought to the joyful and mundane events in her life, she invested in her suffering as well.

COMPLICATIONS OF MOURNING ASSOCIATED WITH LONGEVITY

The gift of longevity is a mixed blessing. There is no question that, in general, the life cycle is growing longer, healthier, more active, and richer in opportunities and experience. However, along with this rich gift, uniquely painful losses, which were often rare or unknown in the past, are now becoming common. Moreover, the character and quality of these losses tend to complicate the nature and the outcome of the mourning process experienced by the bereaved.

Severe Mental Impairment in the Spouse

When decline is mental rather than physical, the process of mourning is prolonged, as well as complicated. In the early stages of impairment, the affected spouse is aware of serious changes and is mourning for him or herself in a parallel process with the spouse who is the caregiver. As normal abilities in personal care and social skills begin to deteriorate, early losses involve lost activities, future plans and social relationships. As more severe symptoms develop, the healthy spouse becomes parent, caretaker, jailer, and nurse, and the affected partner is progressively unable to fill any normal marital functions. Partners who have watched their mates deteriorate drastically describe their feelings as "a rehearsal for mourning" or "the 20 year funeral." Their lives enter a state of limbo in which they can identify no real beginning and no end.

Care of the affected spouse assumes the central position in the caretaker's life and begins to require an ever more significant proportion of emotional and physical commitment. Understanding the disease that has caused this deterioration may be one of the few activities outside of caretaking that caregivers can allow themselves. This is probably a positive and indirect form of mourning in which the grieving spouse, rather than focusing on the lost love object (the sick spouse), focuses on the disease and the process of defeating the disease through the intellectualized and executive functions of forming supportive organizations, raising money, and establishing service networks specific to the spouse's problems.

Alzheimer's Disease accounts for a large percentage of severe mental deterioration seen in older people. It is progressive, incurable, and usually has a lengthy course (10 to 20 years). During that period, the patient first suffers relatively minor memory loss, which progresses in severity, impaired judgment, personality change, and often violent and agitated behavior. Wandering is common and the patient cannot be left alone. The end stages of the disease are characterized by severely regressive behavior, as the deterioration of the memory appears to destroy even some of the earliest instinctive behaviors, such as chewing and swallowing.

Other illnesses, such as stroke, arteriosclerosis, and Parkinson's Disease, can result in significant mental deterioration. They differ in course, intensity, and most important, duration. Damage is often limited to certain areas of functioning, and the possibility exists for arresting the deterioration, treatment, and rehabilitation. Alzheimer's Disease, thus far, offers none of this hope. All that can be done for Alzheimer's victims is to maximize functioning for as long as possible. Unfortunately, the day will arrive when the patient does not know those closest to him or her, and all of the marital relationship will have disappeared, except that which the spouse keeps alive in memory or in fantasy.

Lengthy, Painful, Expensive Death Process (Pulling the Plug)

Feelings of anger, guilt, and fear are aroused during a lengthy, painful, and expensive death process. These feelings are intensified when there is a necessity of deciding to continue treatment, or using life support machines. When the process of dying is difficult, negative feelings are generated on several levels: that the dying person and the family must suffer so, and that the family resources (financial, emotional and otherwise) are being depleted. Dreams of togetherness, present relational needs, and plans for the future must be abandoned or drastically revised. The anger is often intense and followed by guilt, since social values dictate that anger in these situations is not acceptable. The whole process is further complicated by the fear of expressing the anger, especially to the dying relative, thus forcing indirect and projected channels of expression.

Fear is another dominant emotion at this time: fear of losing the loved one; fear that the loved one will not die, and fear that a long, painful death could happen to oneself.

As we have seen, guilt, anger, and fear are feelings that are highly correlated with a pathological or a blocked mourning process.

Death of an Adult Child

The death of a child is viewed by most people as life's greatest trag-
edy. The age of the child at death is insignificant, in terms of the
loss felt by the parents. In the parent-child bonding process, a projective identification of the parent with the child takes place; the
parent views the child as an extension of his or her own hopes and
dreams in life. As extensions of parental hopes, children take on important emotional positions in the family and function as parts of
the parent's emotional self. This identification appears to be a normal and inherent part of the bonding process. In a normally functioning family, in which the parents experience themselves as
emotionally complete, this fusion is gradually given up by both parent and child as a part of the maturational and developmental process of the individual and the family. The point is reached where all
family members can regard each other as distinct and separate individuals, yet irrevocably attached, as described by the concept of "invisible loyalties" (Boszormenyi-Nagy & Spark, 1973). It is the
broken bond, with all its past, present, and future promises, that
carries the profound, drastic, and lasting impact of the death of an
adult child.

The following are the major emotional issues in mourning the
loss of an adult child.

1. *Identity Issues.* The projective early identification with the child has
   persisted in a benign form, humorously expressed in the "My son,
   the Doctor" jokes. The aging parent has made an irreplaceable investment of time, physical and emotional energy, and expectation in
   the lost child. These losses are all related to self-image, and negative
   consequences are to be expected.
2. *Sequence (Not the "Right" Time).* In our necrophobic society, a death
   at the "wrong" time (i.e., child before parent) is particularly unacceptable and threatening, because it interferes with the orderly
   transfer of power and responsibility from one generation to the next.
   The aging parents, rather than divesting themselves of responsibility,
   may need to take on some of the responsibilities of the lost child,
   which may postpone mourning indefinitely.
3. *Loss of Control.* With terminal illness, people feel out of control.
   Choice of treatment is one area where some sense of control can be
   maintained. However, when an adult child is the patient, the aging
   parent does not have the power of decision in this matter. Anger may
   be experienced toward the spouse of the adult child for treatment decisions. A further lack of control is experienced with the regression

that both parent and adult child tend to feel. "Mommy" makes it well and "Daddy" takes care of everything.

4. *Guilt Issues.* The feeling of inadequacy experienced by parents provokes a sense of guilt that they have not fulfilled their duty as parents. Guilt is exacerbated if there is a history of a poor relationship. Guilt is also engendered when the aging parents feel concern for themselves. The terminal illness of a child only brings their own mortality into sharper focus.

5. *Isolation.* Society assumes that the loss of an adult child is not as difficult as the loss of a younger child and need not be mourned as intensely or as long, when the reverse is actually more valid. Since the death of an adult child is relatively rare, mourning is further complicated by the lack of support and role modeling from others who have experienced the same loss.

6. *Disturbance in the Struggle for Meaning in Life.* While struggling with the aging process, a view backward and forward in the life cycle is comforting. Margaret Mead (1972) said, "In the presence of grandparent and grandchild, past and future merge in the present" (p. 311). A missing generation skews the continuum. Combined with feelings of isolation, the mourners may feel "cursed by God" or as if they are the recipients of "bad luck."

7. *Effects on the Extended Family Network Relationships.* Members of the older generation feel concern about the loss of valuable family ties and their ability to keep viable relationships with grandchildren and in-laws. This problem is complicated by their concern about assuming responsibilities that they feel unable to undertake.

8. *Lack of Support and Care in Old Age (Special Abandonment).* Older people expect their children to help care for them, emotionally and physically, in times of dependency. With the death of an adult child, they have lost an affective connection and a scarce caretaking resource.

A Female World

With death, the first grief is for the lost person and the relationship with the deceased. These feelings are acute and devastating and begin the mourning process. Secondary losses (e.g., role changes inherent in the loss of a spouse), may be overlooked. The disparity between the male and female lifespan still exists and the average age of widows in this country is 56. Later life is a time in the life cycle when the opportunities to express sexuality and gender reside mainly in the marital tie. Widowers remarry sooner than widows, probably due to the harsh reality that the large numbers of potential wives include the ranks of younger women. In a society that structures its social and recreational ties around the couple, single people suffer greatly from feelings of isolation, inferiority, and loneliness.

Another little-discussed loss results from the extended life span of women. As the aging process continues, the population becomes increasingly female. An important element in the lives of the elderly is changed, on the basic level of expressing their own gender and relating to another gender. As the ratio of men to women drops ever lower, older men find it increasingly difficult to find same sex friends and companions with whom to share activities and social interaction, and women suffer from the homogenization of their environment.

CONCLUSIONS

Crucial to the construction of a model of intervention with older and elderly people is an understanding of the role of loss in the aging process and the effects of loss on the aging organism. Often, failure to engage a client or negative outcome in therapy is directly related to failure to recognize that a loss has occurred and that a mourning process is in operation. We fail to identify loss mainly because, as a society, we are so intent on denying its existence. Loss has come to be synonymous with personal failure. In so negative an emotional climate, it is not surprising that individual perspectives on what constitutes a loss and what constitutes the appropriate reaction to loss are variable and unreliable. Nor is it surprising that therapists may fall victim to such a loaded value system.

Other factors contribute to the failure to identify a grief reaction. Older people often express mourning physically. The qualitative differences, in turn, contribute to the lack of recognition, setting up a vicious cycle that often leads to inadequate or inappropriate treatment. Depression, a common diagnosis in late life, is often not recognized as part of the mourning process, and is treated with medication alone, rather than in combination with psychotherapy to foster a positive mourning process and thus validate choices.

On the other hand, traditional comforts have been lost. The blessing of an unquestioning belief in religion and an afterlife is gone for many of the elderly. The elderly and the dying also suffer from isolation (not individually, but as a group) because they remind us of the passage of time and the finiteness of life. Psychotherapists will begin to see ever greater numbers of clients who are engaged in the process of mourning and who are experiencing the complications of the grief reaction, and they will need to shift their treatment perspectives if they are to provide quality counseling.

9

Restructuring Roles and Life-style: Task-Centered and Action-Oriented Psychotherapy

Almost all mature-stage marital couples requiring counseling have a component of adjustment issues in the presenting problem, and in order for treatment to be effective, these issues must be addressed. Insight-oriented therapy, supportive therapy, and grief therapy are important tools that help couples to understand behavior, to support coping mechanisms, and to promote an effective mourning process. However, it is also necessary to empower couples with the effective tools for the replacement of roles, relationships, and interests that must take place in the successful aging process. The task-centered and action-oriented component of the developmental marital therapy model addresses the issues in marital counseling that require the acquisition of new values, ideas, and skills required during the transitions of aging.

DEVELOPING FLEXIBILITY AND SELF-DIRECTION

There are few positive role models or patterns for growing old. The analogy can be made to getting on a freeway with no directions marked and no signs on the exit ramps. However, if we do not yet have clearly marked directions and patterns, we do have some indications of how to proceed. With the increase in number and rate of changes in late life, a major task is the development of flexibility and self-direction. In the restructuring of marital and family ties for a meaningful and enjoyable life-style for the latter stages of the life cycle, many values, skills, and ideas must be unlearned, or placed in a different priority in the value system. Certain executive or professional skills that have served well in the workplace are disasters in the home, and will not help to develop enjoyable leisure activities.

It is important to begin to challenge ideas and methods that have been very effective in coping in the past, which von Oech (1983) has called "mental locks." For instance, in corporate life, following the rules, being practical and logical, avoiding ambiguity, finding the "right answer," and sticking to what one knows may very well have produced a great deal of success, but how do these strategies work on a highway with no signs? It appears that the values that are little prized in our culture—the ability to make mistakes and to risk appearing foolish—serve much better in uncharted territory. It is the role of the psychotherapist to help the client to build these vital skills and values. And if the client can get a sense of the adventure of this task, so much the better. It is surely incumbent on the therapist to try to instill the joy of the exploration.

There are two major obstacles to the development of flexibility and self-direction: moving past the work ethic and learning to use leisure time. In some ways, these skills are interdependent and develop alongside one another. First, it is necessary to develop new yardsticks for measuring what makes life worth living. Sargent (1980) calls this reevaluation the *awareness phase*, when clients are exploring possible new directions and coming to realize that they can set new goals for themselves. Tasks such as values clarification exercises and brainstorming can be useful in helping clients get in touch with needs for alternate life experiences besides those associated with work. Self-exploration may be encouraged by the introduction of topics such as childhood hobbies or social and political commitments, designed to provoke thought and examination of a rich variety of values and interests. Participation in groups that are designed to explore interests and values is helpful also.

Another rich source of exploratory material that is often ignored is the public library. Developmental bibliotherapy is defined as the use of both imaginative and didactic literature with groups of "normal" individuals, in order to promote normal development and self-actualization or to maintain mental health. Libraries often convene literature groups which, while they may not have the title of bibliotherapy, are actually used as such. Suggested readings, both in literature and didactic ("how-to") materials, can provide valuable role modeling to help discover and promote new interests.

Basically, it is essential to validate the importance of the client's task of restructuring the last phases of his or her life. Any and all methods that cause the client to rethink values and ideas for new life-styles should be introduced as important parts of the therapeutic process.

TASK-CENTERED CASEWORK

During the *commitment and follow-through phase*, when clients are choosing goals and taking steps to fulfill them, is the ideal time to operationalize task-centered casework techniques. Task-centered casework is based on the notion that social work methods are most effective if they are concentrated on helping clients achieve specific and limited goals of their own choice within brief, bounded periods of service (Reid and Epstein, 1972). The helpfulness of brief, goal-directed therapy for older adults is well documented. Furthermore, goal-directed therapy addresses the needs of an older population to have concrete, relatively quick results and to build new skills. The techniques are based on the assumptions that older adults can make decisions for themselves, want to make decisions for themselves, and, in the case of the elderly, need to make those decisions in order to remain functional and independent in the community. People who have their decision-making power taken away from them stagnate and lose touch with themselves and their environment.

Yet, a surprising number of competent, energetic, and creative older people, with few or no complicating problems, run into difficulty mustering the necessary emotional energy to gather information and make decisions. This obstacle is primarily due to the negative views of older people in our society. As Twente (1970) noted, "The self-image and the image of oneself held, or thought to be held, by others always play a vital part in the capacity to use potentials and to be self-directing" (p. 16). When couples are dealing with other emotional problems as well, the result can be devastating and cumulative.

Task-centered casework begins with the assumption that the client knows what is troubling him or her the most, or what he or she wants to work on first. Denying the client's view of the problem only lowers self-esteem and reduces motivation. The role of the therapist is summarized by Reid and Epstein (1972) as determining what the client thinks should be done about the problem and trying to formulate task possibilities consonant with the client's own push for change. In assisting the client in task or goal selection, the therapist has the responsibility of structuring the task so that the chances of full or partial accomplishment are high. The task needs to be explicit and verbalized so that the client understands it. Finally, the task must be structured so that the primary responsibility for reaching the goal is the client's. Once this phase of defining the task is complete, the therapist's primary roles tend to be encouragement and planning.

Case Example

The J Family had a long history of marital and family problems. Mrs. J first requested help to reunite the family when her 28-year-old daughter, who was newly married, indicated that she wished to have nothing further to do with her parents. Mr. J was out of town when the argument erupted and Mrs. J was hysterical, with "no one to talk to." When Mr. J returned, the couple came to the office and gave the following family information.

Mrs. J was 60 years old and her husband was 62. They had moved to this particular city only three months ago. Although they did not say so, it appeared clear that they had moved to be near their daughter. The family had lived on the east coast of America and in Europe for all of their married life (33 years). They both described their daughter as a musical prodigy. Mr. J had always spent long periods of time away from home in the pursuit of his profession, and Mrs. J spent a great deal of her life taking her daughter to music lessons, and even living away from the family residence in order to make appropriate training available to her daughter. Even though Mr. J had little direct contact with his child, he considered her "Daddy's little girl," while Mrs. J appeared to regard her daughter as a friend rather than her child. Both Mr. and Mrs. J agreed that their daughter was never allowed to be a child and that they had always encouraged her independence. Mrs. J felt that her husband had always financially supported the family well, but was never emotionally supportive of her or her daughter. Both partners felt that their daughter had come between them, as all of the arguments that they had ever had were about her. Now, they felt that the crisis with their daughter had brought them together.

In spite of all the information that they supplied, they showed little insight into, or interest in examining, their relationship to each other, and used the therapeutic time to ventilate their feelings of anger and resentment toward their daughter. In order to understand the dynamics of this extremely complicated situation, as well as to evaluate their capacity and willingness to invest in psychotherapy, the therapist initially directed the couple to some family-of-origin exploration. The information obtained was fascinating, both psychodynamically and historically.

Mr. J provided the following family history. He was born during World War I and his mother died shortly thereafter in the great flu epidemic of 1918. He was nine months old at the time and almost died of the flu also. He was cared for by his maternal grandfather's second wife until he was five, when his father remarried. His first memory was at age three when he remembered having an injured hand. The memory of the injured hand was very significant for him, and while he has no memories of severe physical punishment, the importance of the memory suggested the possibility of physical abuse.

After his father remarried, Mr. J's earliest memories were of going to school and of his half-sister, Lily. He recalled her clearly and lovingly, even though Lily was ill and died young. Mr. J remembered that they were friends. He described her as bright and was saddened when she died, as he was "fond of her." Another sister was born when Mr. J was already an adolescent, and he remembered taking care of her, playing ball as she slept in a carriage. It was necessary that he care for the new arrival because Lily had become more gravely ill and she soon died. Mr. J reported that his stepmother never got over this loss, and as a consequence, he thought that his younger sister's life was ruined.

Mr. J's memory of his stepmother was distant and ambivalent. He claimed to have had a good relationship with her, but the emotional tone of his remarks was very cool. The only quality that he could remember about her was that she was a terrible cook. Clearly, he felt like an outsider with her. However, he did know her life history. She was a survivor of the famous Triangle factory fire in the garment district of New York. She came from a rather artistic family of musicians and dancers. One of five children, she had an ongoing close relationship with her siblings. One of her two brothers was the dean of a respected university, and the youngest brother, an artist, lived with the family for a while when Mr. J was young. Mr. J. had rivalrous feelings toward this stepuncle.

Mr. J's father was a tailor by trade and liked to drink. Mr. J considered his father a weakling and they had a poor relationship. He could only remember his father standing up for him with his stepmother once. Mr. J felt that he received no guidance or encouragement from his father, nor did his father pay for his education. The overall picture of family relationships was one of deprivation, loss, poverty, and a lack of intimacy and warmth.

Mrs. J reported a very different, but equally problematic early life. Mrs. J's parents married and had six of their seven children in Europe. Her father was a European agent for a sewing machine company and the family was quite well off. All of Mrs. J's brothers were educated in Russian military schools. There was a 15-year difference between Mrs. J and her next oldest sibling, and Mrs. J had a very painful suspicion that her oldest sister was really her mother. She had never been able to discuss this suspicion with any of her siblings, even though the sister she suspected of being her mother was still alive at almost 90 years old. Some of her memories supported her suspicion. She remembered her mother being very cold and uninterested in her. Although she was given money and music lessons of all kinds, she got no affection from her mother. She remembered being kissed exactly twice in her life. But Mrs. J did remember getting some affection from her sister.

Mrs. J thought that she looked like her father, but had her mother's coloring. She had a very idealized and distant relationship with her father and described him as a "saint." Her father reportedly adored her mother, but her mother did not love her father.

All of the family members were described as very bright. Mrs. J graduated from college at age 18. She met Mr. J when she was 16 and he was her only boyfriend. They married when she was 20 years old. She said she never learned to make friends and never learned to ask for things. Mrs. J thought that she was like her mother, and Mr. J agreed. However, to Mrs. J, being like her mother meant that she had to do three things at once; to Mr. J it meant being "cold."

It was clear that this marriage was a *complementary marriage*, with its foundations secured in replacing some severe deficits of parenting for both partners. Developmentally, the marriage was past the stage of launching children and currently coping with the retirement of the breadwinner. The standard roles and expectations within the relationship were severely disturbed. Neither partner had any understanding of intimacy; in fact, each was terrified of the concept. However, they were somewhat comfortable with their merging and were well adjusted to the conflict caused by the periodic couplings and uncouplings that they required in order to have some sense of having their needs met. Without the stabilizing force of a career and the distance and support provided by their daughter in times of stress, the balance in the relationship was destroyed and the couple was in a great deal of emotional pain. However, they were without the strength or the will to look into their relationship. Therefore, this portion of the counseling process was kept very supportive, with little attempt at obtaining insight into the dynamics of the situation.

The therapist pointed out that one of their more difficult problems was adjusting to a life-style of living in close contact for the first time in their 33-year marriage, without the separations caused by Mr. J's work or their daughter. Thus far, they had been coping with this new circumstance by keeping "as busy as possible." However, while Mr. J was exploring some ideas for teaching on a part-time basis, Mrs. J had resorted to her customary outlet, attempting to maintain close contact with her daughter. This strategy had led to the crisis with their daughter.

The therapist went on to highlight the strengths of the marriage and to initiate some task-oriented interventions. Mrs. J was given the task of identifying her interests. When she had compiled a list of projects that she would like to investigate, she began seeking some educational groups in which she might participate and some voluntary activities of interest. She agreed that her goal would be to have a regularly scheduled program on most days. While most of her activities and interests (such as sewing), settled around the home environment, she located one or two outside interests. Most important, the couple identified their wish to do things together, and they embarked on a program of attending concerts and the theater together, which they had been unable to do in the past because of Mr. J's erratic schedule and the dictates of their daughter's musical training.

Most interesting was the intervention concerning the rift with their daughter. Since the couple had defined their problem as the lack of contact with their daughter, Mrs. J was encouraged to write a letter to the local family service agency where her daughter was residing and request that they contact her daughter to ascertain her willingness to seek counseling for the problem with her parents. Mrs. J felt that this was a satisfactory plan and was encouraged by the prospect of an objective agency becoming involved with her daughter. The daughter did enter counseling, and fairly soon, contact was reestablished, to the joy of her parents. The situation was not smooth, however, and for a period, the therapist served as a supportive figure for the older couple and shared information from the source agency as indicated. In time, as the situation improved, this contact was discontinued and the case was terminated.

CONCLUSIONS

The psychotherapist can play a major role in facilitating the acquisition of necessary skills, values, and interests in rebuilding a meaningful life-style in the latter stages in the life cycle. The very act of taking therapeutic time emphasizes the importance of this issue for the client. First, the therapist must confirm that life-style changes are necessary, and identify the changes that appear to have already taken place in the relationship as well as those that are coming in the near future. Once the need for life-style changes has been verified and defined, the client is helped to formulate the task to be achieved and a plan to accomplish the goals. Finally, the client is supported and encouraged during the process of executing the plan. Task-centered psychotherapy is a vital component of the developmental marital therapy model which affords the clients valuable opportunities to enhance self-esteem through the achievement of definable and measurable goals.

10

Using Ancillary Groups in Marital Counseling with Older Couples

In marital counseling with older couples, a group experience is an especially strong support in the marital therapy process, when used as an adjunct in treatment of specific crises. These crises may be the normal maturational stages inherent in the latter stages of the life cycle, such as the children leaving home, or extraordinary crises, such as the serious illness of an adult child. Older people often experience losses abruptly and in clusters ("the insults of aging"). Self-esteem is under constant attack and as crises dangerously accelerate in number and rate and roles are lost, personal and relational boundaries may get lost as well. The marriage may suffer many negative consequences, one of which may be the development of inappropriate and destructive dependency between the marital partners.

Group contacts, whether in group psychotherapy or ancillary groups, offer older people the opportunity to see that their distress does not signal incompetence or craziness and that their problems are shared by others. Feelings of incompetence and inadequacy are reduced, and valuable opportunities to learn new relational and/or operational skills and to make social and networking contacts are gained. Older people require peer support to sustain their ego image and self-confidence and to anchor them in times of swift transition and social discrimination. Research indicates that contact with peers (especially friends) even outweighs the importance of family interaction in life satisfaction (Spakes, 1979). Groups provide a controlled life experience through the relationship with the leader (if there is one) and through the relationship with group members, as well as offering an ongoing support system for those who need to maximize self-esteem and socially adaptive behavior in the face of problems and crises in aging.

The group method has other advantages in working with an older population. Group therapy has long been recognized as the treatment of choice to reduce resistance, to provide modeling, to decrease feelings of isolation and incompetence through sharing with others who have the same problem, to provide a sense of usefulness through helping others, to decrease dependency and transference on the leader, and to help maintain self-esteem, improve social relations, enhance problem solving, and facilitate adaptation to stress. Williams, Roback, and Pro (1980) specifically related these benefits to their role in maintaining family and peer support. The group experience often allows some of the extraordinary stresses generated in the crises of growing older to be drained out of the marital or family relationship into other appropriate channels. There are a variety of beneficial results. The individual increases the range of options applicable to his or her situation by joining the group, accepts responsibility for resolving the crisis, and brings the new resources back into the marital relationship.

WHEN IS AN ANCILLARY GROUP USEFUL OR NECESSARY?

In addition to individuals or couples in crisis or undergoing serious role changes, clients who have problems caused by inadequate social skills, or who are isolated or alienated due to difficulties adjusting to loss, can be helped to modify their behavior by exposure to others who share similar problems. In addition, clients who need an ongoing support system to reinforce the behavior gains and modifications that they achieved in counseling can benefit significantly from referral to a group experience.

Busse and Pfeiffer (1973) identified group therapy as an important new technique for dealing with depression in older people through sharing with like individuals who have the same problems and helping others in the group, which provides a sense of usefulness. They also found that group therapy adds an actual social group with whom one can identify when membership in natural groups, such as family or work groups, is declining. Shulman (1985) reported on successful group therapy with older women (aged 55 to

75) who had suffered early losses and were unable to tolerate sadness and who used massive denial, somatization, and projection.

The following case example illustrates the use of the group method as ancillary to the individual and marital counseling process. The presenting problem concerns the serious illness of a spouse, which, as we have seen, is a common disruption among older couples and produces enormous stress in the marital and family relationships. In these situations, the roles of patient and caretaker are often new and there is a major shift in long-established relationship patterns. The illness is a transition point in the marital role of both partners which, in some instances, may become long-term or permanent, due either to the nature of the illness or to the reaction of the couple to the illness. Serious illness is a time when the ego is threatened, anxiety levels are high, and the more primitive and dysfunctional defenses are used to cope with the perceived threat to the self: denial, stubbornness, exaggerated independence, and avoidance. These are conditions that increase the normal isolation and depression of both partners that are engendered by a severe illness.

The issue is further complicated when nursing home placement becomes necessary. Society places a high value on keeping a spouse at home for as long as possible. This value is quite naturally reflected in the values of the caretaking spouse and the patient. The problems and conflicts that are created in the process of making the decision can be devastating and destructive throughout the generations of a family. The person who institutionalizes his or her spouse often feels guilt or a sense of personal failure for not meeting all of the spouse's needs. Elaine Brody (1970a) wrote, "The issue has been reduced to institutionalization (seen as negative) versus community living (seen as positive) as though the two plans were inimical rather than different points along a continuum of care and as though alternative community-based services and intermediate facilities exist in sufficient quantity, quality or variety" (p. 44). Unfortunately, these circumstances remain much the same today.

Case Example

A 50-year-old woman requested counseling regarding her mother and stepfather, Mr. and Mrs. B. Three years earlier, Mr. B (aged 83) had been diagnosed as suffering from Alzheimer's Disease. He had had one leg amputated below the knee due to poor circulation and suffered from diabetes and a mild heart condition. Mrs. B's daughter, one of two from her first marriage, was increasingly concerned about Mr. B's deteriorating condition and the stresses placed on her mother. Mrs. B's exclusive activity was caring for her husband and the older couple had gradually lost almost all contact with family and friends due to Mr. B's agitated behavior. Mrs. B complained that her husband's adult children from his first marriage were not interested in him, refusing even respite care, and she was left totally exhausted. She called her daughters repeatedly, crying and complaining, but refused to consider nursing home placement. The present crisis occurred when her husband developed urinary incontinence at night and wet the bed. Mrs. B responded to this new problem by getting up at all hours of the night to change the sheets. She refused to let him wear bladder control briefs.

A family meeting was held with Mrs. B's two daughters, Mr. B's two daughters and one son from his previous marriage, and the elderly couple. Mr. B looked wonderful. His hair was dyed a flattering color and stylishly cut and his clothes were fashionable. He looked 20 years younger than his stated age of 83. He used his prosthesis very successfully indeed, and it was hard to tell that he had one. Mrs. B, on the other hand, though 10 years younger than her husband, looked her age and appeared somewhat dowdy. It soon became clear that Mr. B's appearance was a mirage produced by Mrs. B. He could not follow the conversation, did not understand where he was or why, and did not always recognize his children or his wife. The therapist commented on the discrepancy between Mr. B's appearance and the quality of his interactions. Mrs. B immediately explained that she chose his clothes, dyed and cut his hair regularly, and stood over him for the one to two hours that it took to get him dressed and ready to face the world. The family became silent for a moment and the therapist commented that they did not appear to be aware of the tremendous effort that it took just to get their father dressed in the morning. They were chagrined and wondered why Mrs. B had not let them know sooner the extent of Mr. B's deterioration.

It quickly became clear that Mrs. B was just as frightened of letting them know as they were of knowing the reality of the situation. Mrs. B feared the possibility of having to place him in a nursing home for two reasons: the loss of income from her husband's Social Security check and the loss of her roles as wife and caretaker, and thus her sense of self-worth. After much painful discussion, an agreement was reached that Mr. B needed nursing home care and Mrs. B would enter counseling to help her cope with the imminent changes in her role as a wife and in her general life-style.

The adjustment was extremely difficult. Almost immediately upon entering the nursing home, Mr. B deteriorated sharply, which reflected the extent to which Mrs. B had contributed to his functioning. When she was no longer there to do almost everything for him, it became clear that he was unable to do the simplest personal chore, even with support. Soon, he was unable to use his prosthesis, and the situation steadily declined. Mrs. B reacted with depression and withdrawal from her daily activities. The institutionalization had provoked the resurgence of earlier traumatic events.

Mrs. B had been left a relatively young widow (at age 46) by her first husband. Her children had both left home to marry soon after he died. The close proximity of these events had devastated her and she had felt completely alone, helpless, and hopeless. The trauma of her first husband's death was complicated by the nature of his long series of illnesses. One of the illnesses was a skin condition that was very difficult to care for, disgusting in appearance, and had apparently left him unable to be touched. The overwhelming impression was that for some years before he died, her husband had been her patient and unable to function in any way as a husband. Mrs. B found it difficult to discuss these memories directly, nor could she face her anger in relation to these events, or the nursing home placement of her second husband.

She began spending a large part of her day at the nursing home and complained constantly to the staff and management about the quality and quantity of care that her husband was getting. Within a short period of time, she became a management problem for the nursing home. In individual counseling, she spent the majority of her therapeutic time criticizing the nursing home and began to lose interest in psychotherapy when this problem was not solved. In an attempt to clarify the situation and advocate for the couple, if necessary, the therapist contacted the nursing home social work staff. One of the services offered by the nursing home was a support group for the spouses of institutionalized residents, and a joint plan was made to for Mrs. B for participation in the group, as ancillary to the individual psychotherapy.

The group provided an outlet for some of Mrs. B's guilt and anger through the association with other members who shared the experience of having institutionalized their spouses, and by offering her an acceptable place to complain about the level of care that her husband was receiving. Through group discussions of the experience of role loss and life-style changes, she began to establish a new identity for herself and to construct a new concept of her role of "wife."

Mrs. B's sense of self-worth was bonded to her values of the "good wife and mother." She felt that her role was to provide caretaking to all members of her family, to be polite, sweet, and strong. She found it impossible to ask for help or to vent her feelings directly. Anger and other expressions of negative feelings had no place in her value system and therefore, she was extremely threatened and experienced overwhelming anxiety when she became aware of any of these feelings. However, as long as the verbalizations of the events and feelings were kept within the limits of her value system, she could ventilate negative feelings indirectly and received a great deal of relief from doing so. As she saw others in the group express anger and resentment, not only at the nursing home, but at family members, and even the affected spouse, she began to feel more free to express these feelings also.

With the support and validation of the group members, Mrs. B. was able to recognize that she had defined the task of frequent visiting and quality control supervision as the new marital tasks that defined and maintained her role as "wife." This new concept was validated by the group, but the methods and standards that she used as criteria were confronted. All of the members of the group were able to share their experiences and impressions of the care provided by the nursing home, and a consensus was reached that, while all agreed that the care could and should be improved, it was at least adequate and perhaps even a little better than that. The group members began to discuss strategies for achieving some of their goals in improving the care offered. As a result, some of the members joined a local organization whose objectives were to improve the standards of local nursing homes.

When this process was well under way in the group, the members began to discuss their marital status. They felt that they were in limbo, married, but not married. They began to identify the specific losses that they were experiencing. Mrs. B brought these issues into individual psychotherapy and began the serious business of mourning her losses. As she mourned for past and present events, she began to share concern about her own health. Several years before, she had been diagnosed with cancer of the bowel. She was successfully treated with surgery, but still required yearly checkups. Because of the difficulties with Mr. B, she had not been to her physician for two years. She was very frightened, but scheduled the necessary tests and appointments. To everybody's great relief, she got a clean bill of health.

She gained some feelings of mastery over her new situation during the process of reviewing her course of action and accomplishments after the death of her first husband and her children had married. She had found a very creative antidote to her feelings of rolelessness by becoming a housemother in a fraternity; she left this job after she met and married Mr. B. She described the marriage as successful until her husband became ill, and expressed awareness that the options that had been open to her the first time that she was widowed were no longer available or appropriate. For one thing, she was not really widowed and furthermore, she did not think that she had enough strength to keep a job. However, reminiscing about how she coped previously, together with the recounting of her successes and the role modeling that she received from the other members of her support group, definitely began her process of accepting the need for the nursing home placement and opened up options for the future.

During six months of treatment, Mrs. B never stopped mourning her lost status and loneliness. But, by termination, she was able to identify and deal with the issues of the present and the future, her fear of widowhood, of loss of independence, and of death. Without the use of the ancillary group, Mrs. B would have gotten stuck at the very beginning of the therapeutic process and left treatment, as her anger and guilt mounted to intolerable levels. The outcome would very likely have been negative for her husband and for herself.

PROBLEMS IN GROUP WORK WITH OLDER ADULTS

Group psychotherapy with older adults is a difficult technique to employ both from the perspective of the client and the leader. Older people are more reluctant to express personal issues in a group. In addition, attempting to solve problems through the group process is often alien to them (Altholz, 1973). On the positive side, groups focused on older adults often have members ranging in age from the 60s to the 80s. This variety is a benefit because it provides an experience of differential maturation to the group members. However, group continuity is threatened by practical considerations such as high absenteeism due to illness, lack of transportation, and unwillingness to discuss appropriate issues (Altholz, 1973). In order to overcome these obstacles, psychotherapy groups serving older people need to be open-ended and each session should be self-contained (i.e., no specific agenda should be carried over from one meeting to another).

The group therapists must determine what role the leaders will fulfill for the group. They may be passive, functioning as listeners and targets for the ventilation of the members' feelings, or active, assuming the role of teacher, facilitator, questioner, consoler, and moderator. Often, the purpose of the group will help determine the role of the leader. Two leaders are often preferable to one. The mild impairments of the members and the difficulty of the topics discussed (e.g., death, loneliness, etc.) make it difficult for one person to sustain the enthusiasm and the energy, both physical and mental, necessary to lead a group (Goldfarb, 1971).

Countertransference issues are common, precisely because of the difficult issues discussed and the dependency of the clients. The therapist faces a lack of narcissistic gratification, the need to accept the idealizing and the rage of the members, the fear of one's own aging process, and a tendency to rescue the members. For these reasons, it is often not appropriate for a therapist to have the same clients in marital therapy and group therapy at the same time. (It is also not beneficial for clients, as one of the major reasons for referral to a group is to dilute the dependent transference encouraged by the one-to-one therapeutic relationship.) This issue is less important when the referral is to a time-limited self-help group or a group with an educational focus, in which the therapist interacts with the group in a different mode. In these instances, the determining criterion for the therapist accepting members to the group from their marital counseling clientele would be the level of dependency exhibited by the clients.

GROUP MODALITIES

There is a great proliferation of groups dealing with a variety of emotional and psychological issues, and with significant differences in definition, goals, methodology, and composition. This is largely a by-product of a mobile society and the fragmentation of traditional support networks, such as the family, the church, and the neighborhood. Group modalities range from the highly structured traditional group psychotherapy to drop-in discussion groups, with a wide range of interim structures. With so many options, appropriate referrals can be made to more than one kind of group, if indicated. An appropriate choice can make a major difference in the course of the marital therapy and the prognosis of the clients.

Group Psychotherapy

Group psychotherapy refers to regularly scheduled, voluntarily attended meetings of acknowledged clients with a trained leader for the purpose of working through various aspects of the client's functioning, and developing the client's healthier and more satisfying potentials (Altholz, 1973). This definition does not make reference to the age of the group participants. The resolution of problems through the group process is the same for all ages. The only difference lies in the rules governing group interaction between groups with an older clientele and groups with a younger clientele. The younger groups discourage out-of-group contact, whereas the older groups encourage it, for the perhaps obvious reason that older people need the social supports gained in the group to replace decreased social contacts.

Reminiscence Groups

Reminiscence groups are similar to psychotherapy groups, without the title or open identification. Writing and telling reminiscences in groups permits older adults to deal with strong emotional issues in a controlled and focused manner under the auspices of a trained leader. It allows the participants to relive their triumphs and reminds them of coping devices that have served them well in the past. Individuals resolve old issues and hurts in the process of remembering and reliving the circumstances of their lives. They have the opportunity to deal with angry and hurt feelings with the support of other people who share similar knowledge and value concepts and to explore powerful developmental themes (Getzel, 1983). The process appears to have long-term, as well as short-term, benefits. Participants of a reminiscence project in a nursing home showed improved short-term memory and expressed happier feelings about their lives (Psychology Today, 1985, p. 8).

Self-Help Groups and Support Groups

Self-help groups or support groups have emerged and spread to address unmet needs, serve neglected populations, or offer a different, nonbureaucratic kind of help. They are made up of people who help each other and in so doing, help themselves, a kind of two-way volunteering. They share a common concern or problem. They meet regularly, with a specific focus, in order to share their experiences and find ways to cope with problems, relying on their individual and collective knowledge and skills. Most self-help or support groups arise spontaneously and develop a democratic self-governing structure, although some are affiliated with a national organization. Alcoholics Anonymous is an example of a self-help group that is so successful that it is widely recognized as a necessary partner in the treatment of alcoholism (Lidoff, 1984).

However, psychotherapists have often started support groups or self-help groups to answer unmet needs. Traditionally, when support groups are led by psychotherapists, it is usually because the group has been founded by the professional. In a self-help group, the leadership role usually focuses on facilitating interaction among group members, providing supportive service to enable the group to continue to function (for instance, the meeting place), recruiting new members for the group, consultation, and serving as a link to traditional services.

However, as successful as many self-help or support groups have become, they have some limitations. They are often loosely structured and informal and thus may fail to provide continuity for a person in need of help. Often, professional services are needed in addition to, or even instead of, a support group.

Training Groups

Groups that provide specific skills training, such as assertiveness training, have a great deal to offer in terms of new and necessary knowledge. Also, they build self-esteem and they tend to be fun. They focus on creating mutually respectful social interactions through modeling, role playing, and positive feedback or reinforcement. Training groups usually have specific objectives, emphasize the positive, are brief and economical, can be utilized and understood by a wide variety of persons, teach skills that generalize to many problems, can be used in a natural environment, and can be taught by paraprofessionals. An excellent example are groups that train peer counselors for the expediter roles. Older and retired persons can be an effective corps of counselors for the elderly because of their interest and understanding of the issues and problems of growing older (Sargent, 1980).

Educational Groups or Classes

Education is often a part of the therapeutic process but rarely acknowledged as such. Family life education has lately become an important component in psychotherapy services offered in social service agencies and by private practitioners, due to the recognition that many clients' needs were not being met by counseling alone. The educational format was found to be preventive in nature, to provide valuable training in human relationships, and to be a non-threatening arena in which to work with clients and potential clients (Sargent, 1980). These attributes make the educational format ideal for older clients.

Educational groups are invaluable in providing information for older adults who are at the frontiers of a new life experience. Never before have so many people reached such advanced ages. We are only beginning to understand the implications for society and for the older people themselves, who must live these years, hopefully with some dignity and some pleasure. Any increment of information is essential in this goal. Classes and educational groups offer new stimulation, new friends, and the opportunity for intellectual and emotional growth. Informal classes and groups can get discussions going that share views on the myths and facts of aging, the meaning of retirement, changing family relationships, and community facilities for volunteer work. These groups are already important adjuncts in building a meaningful life for older adults, and as the level of education among the elderly increases, they will increase in importance.

Advocacy Activity Groups

Participants in social action activities that benefit older adults as a group gain social and psychological benefits beyond the immediate goals of the program. Older people know their own problems, they vote in large numbers (and thus have a power base), and they are the best resource to speak on their own behalf. Participants have the opportunity to develop and exercise their leadership skills and to enhance their status and sense of self-worth (Duhl, 1983). People never before involved in this type of activity seem to enjoy the stimulation and experience that it offers. Advocacy groups even attract men, who are traditionally more difficult to involve in typical senior activities than are women. The success of these groups points out the need for meaningful roles for older adults in our society. As more and more women retire from the work force, the entire senior adult population will share the characteristics now associated with retired men. Senior adult programs that are largely recreational will not meet their needs.

CONCLUSIONS

One reason that counseling and psychotherapy have not had the same results with an older clientele as with a younger population has been the incompatibility between the model of service delivery demanded by traditional approaches and the specific characteristics and problems of older clients. Traditional models are problem-oriented and view clients as diseased. Older clients, whose self-esteem has been under attack, whose competence is viewed as suspect, and who have strong dependency issues, find it difficult to place themselves in a role that reinforces these threats. The addition of an ancillary group experience as a part of psychotherapy effectively addresses these very important issues. Participation in a group is an empowering experience and dilutes the dependency inherent in the individual psychotherapeutic relationship. A group can offer a corrective recapitulation of the primary family group by serving as a "good family" for persons who feel alienated from their own families. The group experience reduces isolation for a person facing a difficult situation and offers them a new kind of relationship to professionals, who are no longer helpers of the helpless, but collaborators with group members. Participants gain a sense of usefulness through helping each other (Busse & Pfeiffer, 1973). For older or elderly people, these issues are integral to the tasks of their developmental stage and resolution is central to a positive psychotherapeutic outcome and to a successful aging process.

PART III

Facilitating the Use
of Psychotherapy with
the Aging Population

11

Special Issues and Problems in Psychotherapy with Older Individuals and Couples

Because of obvious emotional difficulties, the barriers and problems inherent in the latter stages of the life cycle, and the growing size of the older population, it would seem that older Americans should account for a large proportion of clients in psychotherapy. Instead, they have been underrepresented and underserved by the helping professions. Furthermore, the development of models and techniques to meet their specific psychodynamic needs has also suffered. There are a variety of reasons that account for this situation: historical perspectives, the resistances inherent in the aging process, and the different tools and dynamics involved in working with older people. Moreover, in counseling, these clients are often dealing with irreplaceable losses such as physical deterioration in themselves and their loved ones, and focus on mourning, death, and dying.

These issues force therapists to face their own, perhaps unwelcome, aging process. Rubin (1977) has examined the problem from the perspective of the counterproductive attitudes of the therapists, citing pessimistic theoretical opinions, countertransference feelings, educational deficiencies, and cultural biases. However, while these issues are very important, they do not completely account for the problems encountered in working with an older population. It is also necessary to examine the effects of cultural attitudes on the cli-

169

ent and on the therapist as well; the role and uses of resistance for the clients; transference and countertransference issues; and some real differences in therapeutic process and style, for which we have little preparation.

CULTURAL BIAS

We are a youth-oriented society that values productivity and financial success, equates wealth with virtue, and uses the national celebration of sex to sell the variety of goods that we produce. It is not difficult to understand that as a young country in the full spate of power, our national identification is with the values of youth. However, these values tend to exclude older people from participating in the mainstream of our culture. Older people no longer educate their young into a profession, and indeed what they know, especially about science and technology, is often obsolete. As the useful knowledge base to be exchanged between the generations has decreased, cultural bias has exacerbated the development of negative attitudes toward older people. Most recent cultural attitudes categorize the elderly as burdens or as problems requiring solutions. These values and attitudes have a direct effect on the younger population, leading them to reject their own aging process. Combined with these issues, there is a waning historical sense too, which increases the sense of isolation in society.

As the numbers of older people have expanded in recent years, ageism has caused serious problems for the elderly themselves, for their families, and for our society. Rapid technological and social change has robbed older people of many of the important roles and tasks that they filled in the recent past. Although we generally espouse the view that technological advance has overwhelmingly positive benefits for society, one serious negative effect is the destruction of the natural, normative position of older people in our society. Another serious negative consequence is that medical technology, in the course of finding cures for many diseases that made death a familiar part of living, has taken illness and death out of the home and into the hospital. Thus, death has become increasingly unfamiliar and unacceptable. For instance, death among children was once a common event, whereas today it is relatively rare. While no one would wish to return to earlier rates of mortality, the rarity of death does place more stress on those who are facing death.

Jung (1964) has identified death as the central problem of the latter half of life, as sex is in the first half. Obviously, this segregation of death is a new development in the life cycle. Death used to be spread out among all the generations, whereas today, we have succeeded in virtually banishing it to the latter stages of the life cycle. There are even hopes of banishing death altogether; we have an enormous amount of research funds committed to lengthening the life cycle, and attempting to defeat death. Death has come to be a symbol of technological failure and the result is a cultural attitude that has been described as *death anxiety* or *death phobia*. Greene (1986) describes death anxiety as a major obstacle in the provision of services to older and elderly clients. Both therapists and clients know that they will be thinking about and discussing death, a threatening topic to both, if they engage in the therapeutic process.

Therapists and older people are members of the society in which they live and live by the values and mores of that society. Therefore, older people have a major task in sustaining self-esteem in a society that does not esteem them because of their lack of material productivity and wealth, and which finds them a threatening symbol of failure as they approach death. Therapists must overcome not only their feelings of countertransference, but the suspicion that the work that they are doing may be second rate by its association with a second-rate clientele, and may even be damaging to their professional aspirations. Mental health theories, techniques, and practitioners have been under attack and are still not always accepted as bona fide members of the scientific community. This issue is often expressed in the lack of acceptance and trust among the different disciplines practicing psychotherapy, and makes it doubly difficult for psychotherapists to associate with another "underdog" for fear of further weakening claims to valid professionalism.

These are the basic cultural and social issues that have impacted so negatively on the provision of mental health services to older adults. They have served as the foundation for resistance issues from both the client and the therapist and have colored the transference and countertransference patterns in the therapeutic relationship.

RESISTANCE FROM THE CLIENT

Older clients have a reputation for unwillingness to use psychotherapy and resistance in the therapeutic process. They have traditionally been regarded as nonpsychologically minded, inflexible, unmotivated, and unable and unwilling to pay for services. These concepts have some validity. Twenty years ago, many older persons who came to the attention of social service agencies were foreign born, uneducated, and poor. There is no question that they were not psychologically minded and were unable and unwilling to pay for therapy. That generation is rapidly disappearing, yet the unwillingness and "resistance" to psychotherapy have not. How can we explain this ongoing phenomenon now?

The Positive Functions of Resistance

Basic to understanding this issue is the redefinition of our view of resistance. Resistance is generally taken to pertain to counterproductive therapeutic interactions, initiated by clients in order to avoid working on their problems or in order to protect dysfunctional patterns of behavior. With older people, resistance has a more positive function. A great deal of the behavior that has been labeled "resistance" is behavior directed toward the protection of the more functional self. As older people are coping with rapidly occurring losses of their physical and mental functioning and of supports in their social system, they struggle to maintain independence and competence. They fear the inherent dependency that is involved in the psychotherapeutic relationship. Furthermore, the stresses in the latter stages of the life cycle provoke dependency needs in the elderly and resistance may be viewed as a containment measure for dependency needs (Brink, 1979).

Unwillingness to enter the therapeutic contract may also be a direct coping response to the negative attitudes of aging. Many older and elderly people have a psychologically healthy unwillingness to expose themselves to relationships and situations that will be viewed negatively by members of their support system, and resistance may be viewed from this perspective as protective of their fragile and constantly attacked sense of self-esteem. This difficulty usually gives way when therapy is presented in a nonthreatening format, such as a class, or in a nonthreatening setting, such as a senior adult center.

In addition, older people are aware that they will need family support more and more as the years progress. They begin a functional process of moving closer to family members who will be prospective future caretakers. At the same time, they attempt to maintain their position of worth and power in the family. One of the ways that they attempt to do this is by problem sharing with the family—that is, "you help solve my problem and I'll help solve yours." This approach produces interdependence without loss of respect and worth within the family. There is a resultant natural reluctance to take problems outside of the family system, for fear of both offending potential supporters and of losing face.

The problem of financial resources also contributes to resistance. Older people, with good reason, tend to regard their environment as threatening and aggressive and to view themselves as inadequate. One potent way of maintaining a sense of adequacy is to maintain control over money. Older people are also very concerned with the loss of resources. New sources of income are usually not forthcoming for the retired; in fact, retirement usually decreases income. Many older people are concerned about their ability to maintain their life-style and fulfill retirement plans. More than likely, they have suffered an illness, or have seen a friend suffer an illness, and the reality of the enormous cost of health care has become an ever-greater concern. Some have great fears of running out of resources and most have a reality-based concern. Thus, many older people, who may also have little or no mental health care insurance, are reluctant to spend money for psychotherapy. Fortunately, the latest changes in Medicare mental health care coverage will make psychotherapy and counseling somewhat more accessible to those over 65.

Finally, older people who may be in need of psychotherapy are often functional individuals whose coping devices have broken down under intolerable stress or crisis. Their unwillingness to seek psychotherapy may be viewed as valid confidence in their own power to overcome their difficulties, based on their past history of success in doing so. They may eventually seek psychotherapy for help, but it will take them longer to do so. This delay can have very positive dividends for the therapeutic relationship.

Case Example

Jean reported that she had periodically telephoned, but hung up without identifying herself, for a year before making an appointment. She was attempting to cope with an extremely difficult and resistant depression that her husband had been experiencing for five years. Before she was able to enter into the therapeutic contract, the marriage was almost totally destroyed and her own sense of self-worth had deteriorated drastically. Both she and her husband had tried exhaustively to solve their marital problem, unfortunately only sinking themselves deeper and deeper into the pit of depression. Jean even began to use alcohol as a sleeping medication. This latest development frightened her and finally convinced her that the solution was beyond their unaided capacity.

Jean alone made the request for service, and initially she was seen on an individual basis. However, before long, it was clear that her anxiety and use of alcohol were in large part due to the marital breakdown and her reaction to her husband's depression. He agreed to come to one session, but with the clear understanding that he was merely helping with his wife's therapy. When asked to participate in marital counseling, he showed a great deal of anxiety and also some awareness concerning the dependency involved in the therapeutic relationship. Because of this issue, he would only agree to provide marital and individual history and limited participation. He was able to come for some individual sessions and occasional joint sessions. For the most part, he participated in therapy by being supportive of his wife's therapeutic process and learning from her.

The couple made unusually rapid progress. The husband was able to share his depression with his wife, and she learned to tolerate his expressions of sadness and regret without trying to fix his problems for him or taking responsibility for his unhappiness. She also learned to take more responsibility for decision making. The positive aspects of the relationship soon took over and cleared the path for him to deal with his depression.

This case demonstrates that once the positive functions of resistance are understood and placed in proper perspective, strategies for overcoming them or working creatively with them can be crafted.*

THE RELUCTANT THERAPIST

Robert Kastenbaum (1964) coined the phrases "the reluctant therapist" and "the helpless helper" in discussing professional disinterest in working with the elderly. He revealed that the typical psychotherapist appears to represent faithfully the basic discriminatory attitudes in our society. Older clients have been viewed as poor investments of time and energy, as they have relatively little time left to live. The resistance of the clientele and their lack of insurance or other resources for payment were also noted.

Rubin (1977) identified two other issues of equal importance: educational and clinical deficiency and pessimistic theoretical opinions. Negative attitudes have led to serious gaps in research and

---

*This case example is described in greater depth and detail in Chapter 7.

education about the aging process and normal behavior in aging. Psychological changes intrinsic in the aging process have added to pessimistic opinions. For example, the older person's fear of change and slower reflexes and thought processes are often labeled as inflexibility, and many professionals have concerns that the older person's psychological mechanisms have been hardened by age.

From the earliest stages of development in the helping professions, our thinking about theoretical models for treating the elderly has been curtailed. Freud (1924) began this process when he said that old people were not accessible to his therapeutic methods. The rationale for psychotherapy with older and elderly people was that they had limited time and resources to give to psychotherapy and that their behavior was goal directed and oriented toward problem solving and therefore, psychotherapy should be brief and problem centered (Goldfarb & Turner, 1953; Meerloo, 1961, and Brink, 1979).

Changes in Therapeutic Boundaries and Style

Brink (1979) also discussed the changes in pace and style necessary when working with the elderly. He recommended a slower pace, accompanied by an active, eliciting interaction with the client. Blazer (1982) suggests speaking clearly, slowly, and in concrete terminology. He also discussed the need for nonverbal communication, such as touching, and the necessity of tolerating many missed sessions due to illness. Although these recommendations refer mainly to the elderly, they are valuable suggestions in learning to work with an older clientele in general. However, these techniques can violate the most sacred client-therapist boundaries, leaving professionals feeling very uncomfortable and questioning whether the relationship has left the realm of professional psychotherapy and entered the murky world of paid companionship or semiprofessional behavior. Only recently, new thinking has begun to provide the theoretical concepts that account for the alterations necessary in the conventional boundaries of the client-therapist relationship.

The major differences involve touching (even kissing and hugging), personal sharing, receiving gifts, and adapting to the complicated active role that the therapist often needs to assume. Elderly people, in particular, are often starved for *touch* and for signs of affection. They often live alone, and even though they may have loving and involved family members, the number of opportunities for being affectionately touched are sharply limited. They are in need of this touching from the supportive people in their environment and respond well within the therapeutic contract to touching and hugging and will often deliver kisses as well. While kissing and hugging should not be initiated by the therapist (nor is it necessary to respond, if it feels uncomfortable), touching and, at times, holding the client closely is definitely recommended as a valid and, at times, necessary communication tool.

Personal sharing is another area of interaction within the therapeutic relationship that has a different meaning for the older adult. Almost all older adults have lived through varied, and at times, quite difficult life situations. They are aware of having a store of wisdom about life events and often have a sense of mastery in specific areas as well. The client's request for personal sharing from the therapist appears to be the quite straightforward wish to maintain self-esteem through the establishment of some common ground, such as the knowledge of shared life experiences, and a way to define the self in relation to the therapist. As such, request for personal sharing should be responded to simply and without embellishment. If the request has a deeper meaning, it becomes apparent almost immediately and then needs to be dealt with in the standard manner.

Gifts are often offered by an older population. The exchange of nonmonetary gifts (e.g., therapy for food, perhaps) appears to enhance the acceptance of the "gifts" of therapy. Gifts represent an exchange of nurturance that maintains equality in the relationship and defends against excessive dependency feelings.

To return to the case example cited earlier in this chapter, at one point, the therapist was making a representational outline of a concept for the client. The client remarked that it would be easier to see on a blackboard and the therapist agreed. Not long afterwards, the client appeared with a small used chalkboard, perfect for the size of the office. It was accepted, hung, and often used in the course of therapy. There is no question that it was a symbol of this client's active and nurturing contribution to the therapeutic process. Usually, however, the gifts are food—a special cake or a sample of a holiday dish—or flowers from the garden. Occasionally, gifts are purchased, and when this occurs, they are almost always token gifts that clearly state their benign purpose.

Finally, there is the *active style* required from the therapist. Older clients do not respond well to the silent therapist who waits for the client to fill the space. There is a high level of dependency needs on either end of the cycle, which require fulfillment if the client is to function at maximum capacity in the psychotherapeutic relationship. The covert dependency needs of the older and, especially, the elderly client are met, in part, by the active style of the therapist. Since these dependency needs are normal and stage related, the therapist needs to construct a complicated strategy to fulfill those needs. Thus, the therapist often offers suggestions, ideas, and advice and will take a much more active role in setting the agenda for the psychotherapy session. However, this strategy needs to be carefully balanced with interventions designed to maximize the client's participation and responsibility for the process.

All of these approaches are wide departures from hard-learned techniques and often fly in the face of the standard body of knowledge. Working in this way can be a very uncomfortable experience for a therapist, especially an inexperienced one.

TRANSFERENCE

When working with an older clientele, therapists find the transference picture as complicated as other aspects of working with this age group. There are five possible representations: the authoritarian (or parental) transference, the peer transference, the reverse transference, the sexual transference, and the institutional transference.

The Authoritarian (Or Parental) Transference

In the most common transference among the general population, the psychotherapist takes on the parental imago and becomes "as if" he or she were the parent. This transference, known as the authority transference, occurs in all age groups, but within an older group, it often takes place with very dependent clients, and is an acceptable way of expressing dependence. In general, with older clients, the authority transference plays out in a slightly different fashion. The younger client tends to relate to the therapist "as if" the therapist were the good parent (in the case of the positive transference), while the older client relates to the therapist "as if" he or she is an authority figure, who is respected by virtue of knowledge or experience.

Doctors, for instance, are very highly respected by older people both because of their dependence on the physician for health care and because of the almost mysterious knowledge and expertise involved in providing that health care (Brink, 1979). Often, when an authoritarian transference occurs, the client can be influenced to do many things that family and friends could not bring about—for instance, sign powers of attorney or enter a nursing home. Families and psychotherapists are learning to use the authority of the physician to accomplish difficult tasks with elderly family members and are allowing the doctor to be the "bad guy" (i.e., to take responsibility for unpopular decisions).

The Peer Transference

The peer transference is by far the most common transference picture seen with clients in their 50s and 60s, and often well into the 70s. (To some extent, the age of the therapist also has an impact on the transference developed. It is very hard for a 70-year-old client to develop an authoritarian transference or even a peer transference, with a very young psychotherapist.) In peer transference, the client relates to the psychotherapist as a valued equal. Peer transference should not be confused with being overly familiar. The clients rarely confuse it and not only tolerate a good deal of social interaction, but also appear to need it in order to maintain the transference. Eliciting peer transference can be an important strategy in helping clients to maintain self-esteem and avoid resistance (Brink, 1979).

The Reverse Transference

The reverse transference, the second most common transference among older adults, refers to the transference relationship in which the client behaves "as if" the therapist were his or her child (Williams, Roback, & Pro, 1980). It has been noted that this transference is most common among elderly people who feel that their own children have neglected them. This transference gives clients a second chance to get the nurturing that they want from their children. Unfortunately, it is a transference that can elicit a strong countertransference reaction if the therapist feels that the client has failed to accord him or her the proper respect due to a mental health professional.

The Sexual Transference

The sexual transference occurs when the client relates to the therapist with sexual love and seductiveness. It is one of the more troubling transferences for the therapist who works with older client, mainly because of the ageistic notion that older adults should not be sexually active or even interested in sex. This transference may also evoke the unconscious fear of incest in a younger female psychotherapist working with a much older man, and vice versa. Brink (1979), writing from the male therapist's perspective, suggests careful screening of the patients by the therapist as a method of preventing the occurrence of the sexual transference. However, once it has occurred, he suggests dealing with patients' seductiveness openly, by praising their attractiveness, along with making clear declarations of unavailability. In this way, he feels that the expression of seductiveness and sexuality is not stifled, but placed within appropriate boundaries, and therefore rendered nonthreatening to both the therapist and the client. Faye Sander (1976) suggests that declarations of love need to be accepted warmly but without sexual response and within clear boundaries of the professional relationship.

The Institutional Transference

The institutional transference is an excellent transference to foster (Saferstein, 1967). When the client can relate to the mental health care institution as the nurturing parent, peer, or child, the difficult issues involved in loss and dependency can be avoided. The clients themselves seem to sense that this is a positive reaction and it does not take much to elicit this transference, especially when the client is seen through an organization with a high staff turnover. Unconsciously or consciously, the clients seek to avoid the losses involved in connecting to staff members who may not be there in a short while. These clients make their major transference commitment to the institution (i.e., the clinic), which has the indirect benefit of reducing dependency on the therapist, which in turn aids in reducing both resistance from the client and emotional drain on the therapist.

COUNTERTRANSFERENCE

Countertransference has been identified as one of the major reasons that mental health professionals have underserved the older population (Kastenbaum, 1964). In interactional terms, countertransference is a disruption in the communication process of therapy. There is no question that our own fears of aging will be activated when working with older adults, and unresolved conflicts about disability, dependency, and death may surface. There may be a fear of identification with clients who are helpless and feeble and concern about being drained by clients' strong dependency needs. Most difficult, of course, is the case in which the therapist's narcissism is wounded by what he or she views as a hopeless and irreversible condition in the client, and he or she feels like a failure as a therapist.

These are complicated, powerful, and negative issues. A positive past relationship with an older acquaintance or relative can have an ameliorating effect on countertransference issues, but is not likely to banish them altogether. Greene (1986) suggests that they can be managed by self-awareness and supervisory conferences. Coupled with familiarity with older clients and the experience of success in the therapeutic process, the therapist can work through most of these issues.

CONCLUSIONS

For therapists, there is a daunting gauntlet to run before therapy with older clients can even begin. They need to go through an exhaustive self-examination process to identify negative cultural biases and to combat these negative attitudes in themselves, their clients, and others. In addition, the problems of older adults are usually complex and difficult, and the issues presented are often very threatening and frightening, such as physical disability and death and dying. Because of these difficulties, it was not long ago that medication and short-term problem-oriented therapy were regarded as the major tools of therapy in the mental health arsenal for older adults. To some extent, this situation continues to hold true.

Today, therapists are asked to provide a successful experience for clients without adequate knowledge, preparation, and techniques, and often without adequate appreciation from their professional peers. Finally, they often need to recruit their clients. Under these circumstances, it hardly seems reprehensible or even surprising that older adults have been underserved. The challenges are certainly considerable.

And yet, there are significant rewards for therapists who work with older adults. Direct experience with older adults provides a diversity of interaction and relationship that is a stimulus to personal growth and a primary source of knowledge about our roots and heritage. This is a valuable commodity in an increasingly rootless and isolated society. Direct contact supplies us with the information and experience that overcome stereotypes and prejudice that limit interaction with others, and helps to overcome and prevent countertransference reactions. When old people and young people talk together, there is also the educational value of guidance and wisdom about life and insight into the processes involved in accomplishment and achievement.

Doing psychotherapy with older people provides a wealth of professional challenges as well as an opportunity to contribute new knowledge to the field, as fresh and creative strategies are tried and proven. The experience allows for an exercise in mastery, permitting the therapist to accept fears of disability and death, instead of reacting defensively, which is a great release of emotional energy for the therapist. And finally, each client and therapeutic experience present a unique opportunity to garner a rich supply of information and models for a therapist's own eventual "old age."

12

New Directions for the Future

Due to a dramatic increase in numbers, older and elderly people have become normal and highly visible components of the life cycle, in families, in communities, in the arts and entertainment, and in the news. More significantly, older people, along with their issues, joys, and problems, are beginning to assume a growing importance in all levels of our society. This has not always been the case and the position of the elderly in society has been ambiguous, to say the least: at times, powerful and respected, but at other times, a burden and a social problem. Often the aged have been ignored or discarded.

Nevertheless, adequate and clean living conditions, along with the control of many chronic and genetically determined diseases and some age-related diseases, have added many years to life expectancy. One by-product has been the creation of a current group of older people who survive major illnesses and who would not have done so 20 or 30 years ago. These individuals often have significant medical problems and require a heavy investment of medical care, social services, and family support services in order to maintain life.

For all intents and purposes, when most people think of "the old," they are referring to this population. Yet, as human beings reach their fortieth and fiftieth years they begin to experience physical, mental, and psychological changes that are the direct result of their progress through the life cycle, and which are linked to their position in the life cycle, and which are generally referred to as the changes of aging. Thus, we have a picture of incredible diversity in the older population that is almost a contradiction in terms. On one end of the scale, we have healthy, active individuals who may not even be retired from the work force, and who may have no, or only minor, physical signs of growing older; on the other end of the continuum, individuals may be so physically and/or mentally frail that they are dependent on the care of others for survival.

One result of this disparity among the aged is that we have changed our chronological definition of old age. We now refer to the "young old" (up to age 75) and the "old old" (after age 75). The significant growth in the numbers of the *frail* elderly has highlighted the poignant and acute needs of this group, often monopolizing the attention and creative energy of the helping professions, community resources, and private industry. At first, this trend tended to hamper the growth of psychotherapeutic services for older adults. However, parallel developments ensured that the psychological and emotional needs of those in the latter stages of the life cycle would not be ignored.

HOME VERSUS INSTITUTIONAL CARE

As the control of age-related, debilitating disease has improved, individuals with considerable health problems are able to care for themselves, independently or semi-independently. At the same time, changes in family structure, functions, and values are occurring. Older people, including the frail elderly, insist on establishing and maintaining their own homes. This inclination coincides with the personal and public realization that home care is more economical than institutional care and provides a much higher quality of life. The result is reflected in the growth and diversity of services for the elderly now available and developing in the community.

Private industry has not been slow to recognize the profit potentials in providing services for the older and elderly individual and has developed the retirement community, a growth industry, which allows all but the severely frail to remain in the community. Retirement communities often provide meals, shopping service, cleaning, transportation, recreational activities and sometimes even medical services—all on the premises. The major drawback has been the homogeneity of the resident population and the emphasis on physical care and recreational activities as opposed to more diverse opportunities for relationships and more productive activities (e.g., volunteer work). As useful and popular as these communities have been, changes are on the horizon. Older people want to be in the mainstream of the population; they do not want to be sidelined.

Planned communities, with ancillary, supportive services, integrated for all ages, are the direction of the future for living situations.

Homes for the aged are becoming defunct and nursing homes are finding it necessary to provide a highly skilled level of care, in order to be eligible for government reimbursement and to be able to attract residents. The length of stay is decreasing drastically as community services proliferate which allow the elderly and the seriously ill to remain at home. This trend is so marked that the terminally ill, with the help of the hospice movement, are once again dying at home.

These developments have required considerable commitment of time and energy from family members, who are asked to provide emotional support and ancillary services, in partnership with community support systems, for the purpose of maintaining elderly relatives in their own home.

THE CARETAKING GENERATION

Although 80% of the elderly in need of help are cared for by the family (Lebowitz, 1978), the process has been flawed by ambivalence. Subtly influenced by changing laws, which have shifted financial responsibility for the elderly to the government, and prosperity, which supported, allowed, and even encouraged the value of self-interest over the more demanding value of family responsibility, potential caretakers expect to be free of responsibilities after children leave home and many have questioned the appropriateness of providing care for dependent elderly relatives. Other trends may weaken the family's willingness to provide care for elderly dependent relatives or will add to or change the problems that older people face in the future. For instance, families who are now delaying childbirth until the parents are in their late 30s, or even early 40s are creating situations in which the younger generation may have to become the caregiving generation for elderly parents just at the time when they would normally be loosening family of origin ties and leaving home. Such situations are bound to be highly emotionally charged. Most often, however, caretakers have expressed disappointment and confusion at the failure of community institutions to provide adequate care, anger about the need to provide care, and guilt about their feelings. The caretakers began to seek psychotherapeutic help to cope with the negative stresses and feelings involved in providing care to needy family members.

The helping professions first responded to evolving psychological and emotional needs of the older segment of the population within a framework that identified the frail elderly relative as the *problem*. Strategies for easing the burdens of caretaking were devised, along with how-to manuals and publications that validated the ambivalent feelings of the caregivers and supported the need for respite care and ancillary services to enable the caretaking generation of the family to continue functioning.

Slowly, the focus has shifted to an understanding that the *problem is shared*. The caretaker has the psychological problem of deciding what, when, and how much caretaking he or she can, or wishes to, provide and of dealing with the feelings resulting from these decisions. The dependent family member has the problem of obtaining an adequate and appropriate level of care and of being satisfied with it.

The changing structure, function, and values of the family highlighted the enormous stresses involved in growing older and in taking care of dependent elderly family members. As their numbers increased in caseloads, the realization grew that even adult children caretakers were usually older or aged themselves and that a great percentage of caretaking was provided by elderly spouses. It became clear that many issues were shared, such as the concerns of physical dependency, loss, and death. The differences were in degree rather than substance. The caretaker is at the beginning of the process that his or her elderly family member has nearly completed.

There is no question that the plight of the caretaker has made us realize that the stresses in the aging organism are not only biological, but psychological and emotional, and has provided the impetus to rethink our therapeutic position regarding the needs of older and elderly adults. Theoretical developments in the helping professions, specifically the emphasis on families and systems, gave a further stimulus by providing an important role for family history and family-of-origin material in constructing models of psychotherapy.

NEW DIRECTIONS IN PSYCHOTHERAPY WITH OLDER AND ELDERLY ADULTS

One obstacle to the further development of mental health services for the elderly concerns the continued unwillingness of older people to choose psychotherapeutic help for their problems. We have shown earlier that many sources of resistance are positive, self-protective, and realistic reactions to their life situation. The fear of losing control, coping with multiple loss, and dealing with ageism (the negative view of older individuals) produce an unwillingness to participate in any process that may make one less competent to oneself or others. Finally, there are realistic concerns about the costs of mental health care, which is often not covered, or has limited coverage, by insurance companies for those over 65.

In order to make psychotherapy attractive and truly available, new directions and new thinking must include not only new methods of treatment directed at the problems of aging, but strategies for overcoming psychological resistance and the reality-based difficulties of obtaining psychotherapy.

Sargent (1980) describes "nontraditional therapy and counseling," which have the characteristics usually deemed appropriate for the needs of older people. For example:

1. Treatment objectives should be specific and operational, and readily understood by the client.
2. The emphasis is on the positive, and treatment is constructed to be rewarding and successful for the client.
3. Techniques should be usable by paraprofessionals as well as professionals, which greatly increases the number and variety of persons available to provide services.
4. The approaches are relatively brief and economical.
5. They can be understood and utilized by and with persons from a variety of socioeconomic and educational backgrounds.
6. They are effective in dealing with a wide variety of problems.
7. They can be provided in the natural environment, such as the home, schools, and churches.

Sargent does not ignore traditional verbal therapies, but he makes his case for broadening the service base to meet the needs of a larger clientele. All of these points are valid and relevant, not only for brief and nontraditional therapies, but also for use with the conventional psychotherapeutic techniques, when appropriate.

The beginnings of major improvements and developments in mental health services for older adults are already evident. Basic to these changes will be the development of:

1. The outpatient team model of service delivery in conjunction with new and nontraditional sites for delivery of mental health services.
2. Future Models of Psychotherapy:
   a. The development of preventive and stress-oriented therapeutic models.

  b. The sophisticated use of naturally occurring psychological processes.
  c. The increased use of educational and self-help models of intervention.
3. Improved medication and the use of drug therapy in combination with standard verbal therapies to aid mental functioning and in the treatment of anxious and depressive reactions to biological or emotional stress.

The Outpatient Team Approach in New Sites

A creative method of service delivery is to offer psychotherapy as a positive and integral part of established and respected services in a team approach (Cohen, 1983). As the benefits of ancillary health care services become evident in the treatment of physical problems, this model has proved very productive in hospitals and other inpatient settings. It maximizes the effectiveness of all the team members through the regular exchange of information, the reduction of duplicated efforts, and the comprehensive and preventive component of the service provided.

The team approach can be utilized on an outpatient basis with equally efficacious results. We are already beginning to see social workers and psychologists associated with physicians who would normally provide only specialized physical care. The doctor's office is a particularly effective setting. It has the advantages of offering immediate referral, utilizes to maximum effect the positive authority transference with the doctor in the process of engaging the client, and since transportation for the elderly can be a major problem, it offers one-stop care when appointments are synchronized.

Other resistance issues are addressed by the team approach as well. Some professionals, such as doctors and some services, such as medical treatment, are more readily accepted by older adults. For instance, treatment by a doctor, not a psychiatrist, is not negatively viewed by peers and the doctor's services are commonly covered by medical insurance.

Activity and recreational planning for older adults should be formulated in a team approach with mental health professionals who can build in the therapeutic component to the program, provide inservice training to staff and consultation to deal with serious problems and inappropriate participants.

Other efficient antidotes to "resistance" involve not only the change in how and when the psychotherapy service is delivered, but where it is delivered. Perhaps the most important new site for delivery of psychotherapy in the future will be the home. In the recent past, the home visit was a regular feature of the social work and the medical professions. The practice waned because it was not cost effective and it became associated with the less proficient functions of professional practice. For physicians, the high cost in time and energy and the lack of sophisticated portable equipment were clearly the major factors in the cessation of home visits. Currently, some physicians who work a great deal with the elderly are reviving the home visit for those patients who are unable to get to the office. In the process, they are paving the way to dealing with the unsettled cost effectiveness problems involved.

In the social work profession, the home visit was always associated with the delivery of welfare services rather than therapeutic services. As professional training expanded and developed, task and function differentiated. It became acceptable to train bachelor's-level professionals to provide welfare and case management services, while master's-level professionals were trained as clinical psychotherapists and agency managers. Professionals at the doctoral level trained to educate future social work professionals. When the task was psychotherapy, the home visit was dropped because it seemed to lack professionalism, since it was associated with only a bachelor's level of education, as well as being expensive in time and money.

For older adults, we must clearly rethink our positions. Today, older adults are often hospitalized for psychiatric problems, such as depression, because the patient is too physically frail or otherwise unable to come to the office and does not have an adequate community support system to make regular outpatient visits to a psychotherapist possible. Other situations may make home visits the option of choice (for instance, when clients have caretaking responsibilities that do not allow them to come to the office). This issue involved not only the inability to come, but the allocation of scarce time, energy, and transportation resources. Many a client who has the strength and opportunity to leave the house only once a week does not want to use it for yet another errand and the sometimes painful work of psychotherapy. The home visit has advantages in dealing with resistance as well. The home is the client's territory, not the psychotherapist's. This little advantage is often the opening wedge in the establishment and maintenance of the therapeutic contract as the client gains strength and control in a relationship that is, at times, threatening to him or her.

When social work services are offered in ancillary settings, the quality of service often increases dramatically; adjustment difficulties are minimized and maximum use is made of the facility or services offered. Social workers can provide a wide range of services in ancillary settings. They can be involved at all levels of the functioning of the host setting, and provide services to the client from portal of entry to discharge planning. An excellent example is the nursing home. Social workers generally begin their responsibilities with intake assessments, which are invaluable for evaluating the physical and mental functioning of the prospective resident, and also for beginning the orientation process to the new living situation, both for the new resident and for his or her family members. The needs and the strengths of the family, as a whole, are also evaluated in order to head off future problems and to maximize positive family participation in the placement process.

Social work services in a nursing home have a major role in facilitating the adjustment of residents and family members to new routines, rules, and regulations, and in informing in-house staff of appropriate expectations regarding level of functioning of the new resident and their family in the preparation of an appropriate treatment plan.

Direct psychotherapeutic services to residents, old or new, can also be provided. Regularly scheduled interviews offer a valuable opportunity for ventilation of feelings that then need not be directed at family members, who often suffer guilt and may become unwilling to visit as a result. Nursing homes can often be difficult places to visit; the sights and sounds are not always pleasant. When family members suffer from guilt, activated fears of aging, and/or a complaining relative, they often respond inappropriately by either staying away altogether or being overly critical of the institution and its staff. Both attitudes are potentially destructive to the resident and to successful placement. Furthermore, staff responses to residents are, in part, a reaction to family members. Overly critical responses will anger staff and may rebound onto the resident. A neglectful attitude may be even more damaging, as it is likely to be imitated by staff unless the resident has considerable social skills. Appropriately concerned family members who are there to provide emotional support, reassurance that the new resident is not abandoned by the family, and monitoring of the care received are a positive asset to any nursing home and any resident. A social work service helps build this positive connection with the nursing home in a variety of ways, as well as through listening to problems and interpreting the feelings and situations of the resident, the institution, and the family for each other.

Thus, social work services in the nursing home have a role in providing direct psychotherapeutic service to family members as well. Another example concerns the growing number of nursing home placements associated with mental impairment. Group therapy for family members and spouses of the mentally impaired provides a timely and vital service that is essential to successful placement, both for the potential nursing home resident and for his concerned family member, who is often too emotionally and financially exhausted to seek help in a different setting. The group modality, provided at the institution, is particularly efficacious as the members can share information, strategies, and problems. They are able to get a glimpse of the worst and the best the future has to offer, and to know that they are not alone in coping with this most devastating problem. Finally, a social work service in a nursing home can provide on-site in-service training for family members, professional caretakers, and other ancillary professionals responsible for the care of the nursing home resident.

Just as direct service settings for the aging will begin to provide nontraditional opportunities for role and self-esteem building, it will not be long before other settings that supply goods or services to the older citizen will begin to join ranks and add psychotherapy and social work to their range of services (Sargent, 1980). Churches and retirement communities are among the more important possibilities, others include senior adult activity programs, corporations (retirement counseling), Meals on Wheels sites, and health maintenance organizations, to name just a few. For instance, other important sites that will offer psychotherapeutic services in the future will be career management and job placement services and voluntary activities organizations. The development of differential paid and voluntary activity for older adults is an essential program. At present, a great deal of activity made available to older adults is menial and rote—such as card playing and envelope stuffing. The wish to be occupied at something useful is so powerful that any voluntary opportunities are usually oversubscribed. We are beginning to develop some more interesting opportunities, such as helping illiterate adults learn to read, advising small businessmen how to start operations, activities in self-help groups and foster grandparenting programs. Still, much more work needs to be done in this direction, in conjunction with older advisors and mental health consultants.

One area that has not seen growth is paid employment opportunities for older adults. Employment opportunities need an enormous amount of flexibility and short-term commitment in order to be viable. Thus far, this combination of criteria does not seem to have been met very successfully. The unfortunate results are a great loss of work talent to industry and an added tax burden to support those elderly in need of financial aid.

FUTURE MODELS OF PSYCHOTHERAPY

New psychotherapy models for older adults will be preventive in nature and oriented toward the functional person who is undergoing severe stress. The new models will also avoid activating resistance, build self-esteem, offer experiences with new roles, and provide new insights and coping devices explicitly aimed at relevant issues. The educational format will be a very valuable tool, because it can provide valuable information on the physical, psychological, and social processes that older persons are experiencing, role modeling for new and different coping mechanisms, and it can suggest new roles for the future. Most important, the educational format provides a setting to meet other people who are coping with the same problems, which promotes self-esteem through the opportunity to provide and receive role models and ideas from peers.

Naturally occurring psychological phenomena, such as reminiscence and the life review process, will acquire a more sophisticated usage both in traditional psychotherapy models and in nontraditional role building and role modeling activities. New psychotherapy models will likely not be developed specifically for the older or elderly person, but existing and new models will include older people and their special needs.

Some of these techniques will create a ripple effect. As our pool of older individuals who can be interviewed grows, oral history will become a respectable tool in understanding history. Without living witnesses, history has been constructed from documents. Oral reminiscence from the living will provide a deeper and richer dimension to the understanding of current events and of history. In return, these experiences will provide the older individual with new roles in society to validate his or her existence, and will provide valuable roots for families in creating a place for themselves in a society that seems to become more and more impersonal and rootless.

Developmental Psychotherapy Models

Developmental psychotherapy models will be aimed at bridging the gap between esteem building, role building, and stress reduction. These models will provide an opportunity to explore feelings about new roles, while teaching skills connected with these roles. Retirement counseling is a good example. At the present time, retirement counseling is often aimed at financial planning. An effective retirement counseling process would enable the participants to explore their feelings about retirement, decide what they would like to do during retirement, and give them advice and referrals on how to develop the skills to carry out their plans (Sargent, 1980). For instance, an invaluable component of such a counseling process would be a demonstration of how to transfer expertise learned from the work setting to the retirement or semiretirement setting. For instance, a corporate executive can become active in running or supporting his or her local community organizations. However, many can also use help in learning how to change relational skills that were appropriate at work but would be counterproductive at home and in a retired life-style, such as dominating discussion.

Stress Reduction Techniques

Stress reduction techniques will be aimed at self-control of the physical manifestations of stress (e.g., biofeedback) and at learning to reduce stress in the environment. There will be considerable sophisticated developments in understanding and teaching biofeedback, guided imagery, and other allied techniques, and they will be taught routinely in organizations that serve older people. These skills will significantly aid older individuals in learning to keep stress within manageable proportions and will facilitate the activation of their own healthy coping devices in dealing with stress.

Alternatively, as we gradually understand more about the negative effects of stress on biological and emotional functioning, and we begin to appreciate the enormous amount of stress that is a normal component in the late aging process, programs will be developed to reduce stress in the environment. This movement will undoubtedly include changes in laws that concern older people. Laws will be responsive to the differences among older people and, for instance, might allow for earlier retirement for those mentally prepared for it or those physically in need of it, and later retirement for those who wish to continue to work and who evidence the ability to continue to perform satisfactorily. Health insurance could be tailored to suit the new situations which we find ourselves facing; examples would be the catastrophic illness insurance and the long overdue outpatient mental health benefits recently added to medicare coverage.

Some of the moral and ethical issues about death and dying are now being addressed in the courts and by self-help groups. There is little question that with time, all of us will be allowed to make more significant decisions about our own care during terminal and/or debilitating illness, and about how and when we will die. These decisions are going to require a great deal of emotional preparation for dying individuals and their family members, and perhaps for the staffs of the institutions that provide care.

Most important, we will have to find away to validate leisure. In a society such as ours, which values productivity and financial gain to excess, older people may never really feel well about themselves and their role in society unless they are financially remunerated for their activities. This bias is robbing older people of possibilities to contribute to society in ways that are meaningful and esteem building, and is robbing society of resources as well. One approach will be the development of programs involving job sharing, restricted hours, and help with transportation, all of which would allow older people to participate in the work force.

From another perspective, attitudinal changes need to validate leisure. How this will happen is much harder to visualize. Older people may be their own best friends in this regard. As they become more and more prominent in our society, it seems reasonable to assume that their activities will begin to appear more customary and normal and therefore, acceptable and valid.

Improved Drug Therapy

Depression and anxiety are very common emotional disorders among older adults. When coping devices and defense mechanisms break down, severe (possibly suicidal) depressions or anxious depressions are common. In the depths of a severe depression, conventional methods are often not helpful. We have very effective medications which elevate the mood so that the depressed individual can make use of conventional psychotherapy to deal with the real, imagined, or feared losses that have triggered the depression. If medication fails, electroconvulsive therapy is often helpful (Blazer, 1982). However, these treatments are often of limited use with the very people who are the most prone to depressive episodes. In older people, depression or anxious depression is very often triggered by health crises. When these crises involve heart and circulatory problems, treatment may become difficult. Tricyclic antidepressants have a toxic reaction on the heart, which severely limits their use. Other drugs have equally problematic side effects and, in general, older people have unfavorable drug reactions (especially when combined with other medications). Health may be frail enough to rule out even the use of electroconvulsive therapy. New mood-elevating drugs without the negative side effects so devastating to the elderly are desperately needed.

Effective medication, in conjunction with standard psychotherapeutic techniques, can make a significant contribution in the provision of mental health care to older adults.

CONCLUSIONS

The mental health of older adults is going to be in the hands of a team of allied health professionals consisting of the physician (family or internal) and a social work professional in the medical office setting. This partnership is already being seen on a small level and should grow by leaps and bounds in the near future. It is a partnership that will benefit the physician by maximizing the compliance with the prescribed medical regimen, decreasing somatization of emotional issues which may detract from the efficacy of care, and freeing the physician to spend time on the physical problems of the patient.

This approach benefits the patient by allowing the use of psychotherapy in a nonthreatening atmosphere that does not organize resistance, permitting the patient to use psychotherapy through the use of the doctor's authority to make the therapeutic referral, fostering the development of an institutional transference to mitigate loss issues, and helping with the problem of transportation by allowing one-stop health care.

Social workers appear particularly qualified to be members of the team work approach with an older clientele. They have traditionally worn many hats, worked in diverse settings, are familiar with the home visit, and have made their unique contribution to the field of mental health in the areas of systems thinking and environmental manipulation. They are in a unique position to take advantage of skills already at their command and to adapt these skills to a new and challenging area of practice.

The danger in conceptualizing new ideas for working with today's older adult is that the focus will be too narrow. Traditional psychotherapy by itself, offered in traditional settings, does not meet the needs of most older adults. On the other hand, the provision of financial, and other concrete, services, coupled with senior adult activities programs, has also targeted a narrow older population. The majority of older people, facing a stressful and uncertain future, require new and creative approaches that will enhance what is already available and add to it in a meaningful way. Still, when we review the criteria suggested for successful work with older clients, and some of the new developments and ideas for future developments, it must at times appear almost as if we were going backward, rather than forward.

Most theoretical constructs can and should be considered for use with an older clientele, with the understanding that modifications will likely be required. The creative addition of many of the ideas proposed here involves the introduction of therapeutic ideas and skills into the nontraditional arena. The great value of the nontraditional and brief therapies lies not in the expansion of clientele, although this is a valid result. Rather, they are most valuable in their use as a part of a multidimensional approach that enhances traditional psychotherapy and drug therapy in such an increment that, when taken together, the whole is much greater than the sum of its parts. This integration of various approaches is truly the future of psychotherapy with older adults.

References

Ackerman, N. W. (1958). *The psychodynamics of family life*. New York: Basic Books.

Altholz, J. (1973). Group therapy with elderly patients. In E. Pfeiffer (Ed.), *Alternatives to institutional care for older Americans: Practice and planning*. Durham, N.C.: Duke University.

American Association of Retired Persons and Administration on Aging. (1986). *A profile of older Americans, 1986*. Washington, DC: U.S. Department of Health and Human Resources.

Arendt, H. (1959). *The human condition*. Garden City, New York: Doubleday, Anchor Books.

Argles, P. (1984). The threat of separation in family conflict. *Social Casework, 65*(10), 610–614.

Baltes, P. B., & Brim, O. (Eds.). (1980). *Life span development and behavior*. New York: Academic Press.

Barrow, G. M., & Smith, P. A. (1979). *Aging, ageism, and society*. St. Paul, MN: West Publishing Co.

Beck, D. F. (1966). Marital conflict: Its course and treatment. *Social Casework, 67*(4), 212.

Bell, R. R. (1967). *Marriage and family interaction* Homewood, IL: The Dorsey Press.

Bendremer, J. (1983). Bibliotherapy as a tool to understanding and self-growth. *Perspective on Aging*, March/April, *12*(2), 15–18.

Blanck, R., & Blanck, G. (1968). *Marriage and personal development*. New York: Columbia University Press.

Blau, Z. M. (1973). Old age in a changing society. New York: New Viewpoints, A Division of Franklin Watts Inc.

Blazer, D. G. (1982). *Depression in late life*. St. Louis, MO: The C. V. Mosby Company.

Blenkner, M. (1965). Some thoughts on filial maturity. In E. Shanas & G. E. Streib (Eds.), *Social structure and the family: Generational relations*. Englewood Cliffs, NJ: Prentice-Hall.

Bloch, D., & Simon, R. (Eds.) (1982). *The strength of family therapy*. New York: Brunner/Mazel.

Bockus, F. (1980). *Couple therapy*. New York: Jason Aronson.

Boszormenyi-Nagy, I. & Spark, G. M. (1973). *Invisible Loyalties*. Hagerstown, Harper & Row. (Reprinted Brunner/Mazel, New York, 1984.)

196

Bowen, M. (1978). *Family therapy in clinical practice.* New York: Jason Aronson.

Bowlby, J. (1980). *Attachment and loss: Volume III.* New York: Basic Books.

Brennan, E., & Weick, A. (1981). Theories of adult development: Creating a context for practice. *Social Casework, 62*(1), 13–19.

Brink, T. L. (1979). *Geriatric psychotherapy.* New York: Human Sciences Press.

Brody, E. M. (1970). Serving the aged: Educational needs as viewed by practice. *Social Work, 15*(4), 42–51.

Brody, E. M. (1970). Aging and family personality. A developmental view. *Family Process, 13*(1), 23–37.

Brown, B. B. (1982). Professionals' perception of drug and alcohol abuse among the elderly. *The Gerontologist, 22* (6), 519–525.

Brown, D. S. (1980). Age-segregated housing. *Perspective on Aging, 9*(3), 21.

Brubaker, E. (1985). Older parents' reactions to the death of adult children: Implications for practice. *Journal of Gerontological Social work, 9*(1), 35–48.

Brunn, L. C. (1985). Elderly parent and dependent adult child. *Social Casework, 66*(3), 131–138.

Budman, S. H. (Ed.). (1981). *Forms of brief therapy.* New York: The Guilford Press.

Busse, E. W., & Pfeiffer, E. (Eds.) (1973). *Mental illness in later life.* Washington, DC: American Psychiatric Association.

Butler, R. N. (1963). The life review: An interpretation of reminiscence in the aged. *Psychiatry, 26*(1), 65–76.

Butler, R. N. (1974). Successful aging and the role of the life review. *Journal Of the American Geriatric Society, 22*(12), 529–535.

Carlson, C. M. (1984). Reminiscing: Toward achieving ego integrity in old age. *Social Casework, 65*(2), 81–89.

Carter, E. A., & McGoldrick, M. (Eds.) (1980). *The family life cycle: A framework for family therapy.* New York: Gardner Press.

Cath, S. (1965). Depletion and restitution. In M. Berezin & S. Cath (Eds.), *Geriatric psychiatry: Grief, loss and emotional disorders in the aging process* (pp. 21–72). New York: International Universities Press.

Chernus, L. A. (1985). Clinical issues in alcoholism treatment. *Social Casework, 66*(2), 67–75.

Cohen, N. L. (1980). Integrating pharmacotherapy with psychotherapy: The consulting relationship. *Bulletin of the Menninger Clinic, 44*(3), 296–300.

Cohen, R. G. (1983). Team service to the elderly. *Social Casework, 64*(9), 555–560.

Cormican, E. J. (1977). Task-centered model for work with the aged. *Social Casework, 58*(8), 490–494.

Douglass, R. L. (1983). Domestic neglect and abuse of the elderly: Implications for research and service. *Family Relations, 32*(3), 395–402.

Duckworth, G. L., & Rosenblatt, A. (1976). Helping the elderly alcoholic. *Social Casework, 57*(5), 296–301.

Duhl, J. (1983). An advocacy coalition of older persons. *Journal of Jewish Communal Service, 60*(1), 44–47.

Duvall, E. (1977). *Marriage and family development.* Philadelphia: Lippincott.

Engel, G. (1961). Is grief a disease? *Psychosomatic Medicine, 23*(1), 18–22.

Erikson, E. (1950). *Childhood and society.* New York: Norton.

Erikson, E. (1956). The problem of ego identity. *Journal of the American Psychoanalytical Association, 4*(1), 56–121.

Erikson, E. (1964). *Insight and Responsibility*. New York: Norton.

Feldman, L. B. (1979). Marital conflict and marital intimacy: An integrative psychodynamic-behavioral-systemic model. *Family Process, 18*(1), 69–78.

Feldman, L. B. (1982). Dysfunctional marital conflict: An integrative inter-personal-intrapsychic model. *Journal of Marital and Family Therapy, 8*(4), 417–428.

Fenichel, O. (1945). *The psychoanalytic theory of neurosis*. New York: Norton.

Fontane, A. S. (1979). Using family of origin material in short-term marriage counseling. *Social Casework, 60*(1), 529–537.

Framo, J. L. (1982). *Explorations in marital and family therapy: Selected papers of James L. Framo*. New York: Springer.

Freed, A. O. (1984). Differentiating between borderline and narcissistic personalities. *Social Casework, 65*(7), 395–404.

Freud, S. (1917/1961). Mourning and melancholia. In J. Strachey (Ed. and Trans.). *The standard edition of the complete psychological works of Sigmund Freud* (Vol. 14, pp. 237–258). London: Hogarth Press.

Freud, S. (1924). On psychotherapy. In *Collected papers*. Vol. 1. London: Hogarth Press, 249–263.

Getzel, G. S. (1982). Helping elderly couples in crisis. *Social Casework, 63*(9), 515–521.

Getzel, G. S. (1983). Intergenerational reminiscence in groups of the frail elderly. *The Journal of Jewish Communal Service, 59*(4), 318–325.

Gianetti, V. J. (1983). Medication utilization problems among the elderly. *Health and Social Work, 8*(4), 262–270.

Glick, I. D., & Kessler, D. R. (1980). *Marital and family therapy*. New York: Grune & Stratton.

Goldfarb, A. I. (1971). Group therapy with the old and aged. In H. I. Kaplan & B. Sandock (Eds.), *Comprehensive group psychotherapy*. Baltimore: Williams & Wilkins.

Goldfarb, A. I., & Turner, H. (1953). Psychotherapy of aged persons: Utilization and effectiveness of "brief" therapy. *American Journal of Psychiatry, 109*(10), 916–921.

Goldmeir, J. (1985). Helping the elderly in times of stress. *Social Casework, 66*(6), 323–332.

Greene, B. L. (Ed.). (1965). *The psychotherapies of marital disharmony*. New York: The Free Press.

Greene, R. R. (1986). Countertransference issues in social work with the aged. *Journal of Gerontological Social work, 9*(3), 79–88.

Gruen, W. (1977). The stages in the development of a therapy group: Tell-tale symptoms and their origin in the dynamic group forces. *Group, 1*(1), 10–25.

Grunebaum, H., & Christ, J. (Eds.). (1976). *Contemporary marriage*. Boston: Little, Brown.

Guerin, P. J., Jr. (Ed.). (1976). *Family therapy, theory and practice*. New York: Gardner Press.

Gurman, A. S., & Kniskern, D. P. (Eds.). (1981). *Handbook of family therapy*. New York: Brunner/Mazel.

Haley, J. (1973). *Uncommon therapy: The psychiatric techniques of Milton H. Erickson, M.D.* New York: Norton.

Havighurst, R., & Glasser, R. (1972). An exploratory study of reminiscence. *Journal of Gerontology, 27*(2), 245–253.

Hellebrandt, F. A. (1980). Aging among the advantaged: A new look at the stereotype of the elderly. *The Gerontologist, 20*(4), 404–417.

Herr, J. J., & Weakland, J. H. (1979). *Counseling elders and their families: Practical techniques for applied gerontology.* New York: Springer.

Hubbard, R. W., Santos, J. F., & Santos, M. A. (1979). Alcohol and older adults: Overt and covert influences. *Social Casework, 60*(3), 166–170.

Jung, C. G. (1964). *Man and his symbols.* London: Aldus Books.

Kastenbaum, R. (1964). The reluctant therapist. In P. Kastenbaum (Ed.), *New thoughts on old age.* New York: Springer.

Keith, P. M., Goudy, W. J., & Powers, E. A. (1984). Salience of life areas among older men: Implications for practice. *Journal of Gerontological Social Work, 8*(1/2), 67–82.

Kernberg, O. (1975). *Borderline conditions and pathological narcissism.* New York: Jason Aronson.

Kirschner, C. (1979). The aging family in crisis: A problem in living. *Social Casework, 60*(4), 209–216.

Kubler-Ross, E. (1969). *On death and dying.* London: Macmillan.

Leader, A. L. (1978). Intergenerational separation anxiety in family therapy. *Social Casework, 59*(3), 138–144.

Lebowitz, B. D. (1978). Old age and family functioning. *Journal of Gerontological Social Work, 1*(2), 111–118.

Levinson, D. J. (1978). *The seasons of a man's life.* New York: Knopf.

Lewis, M. I., & Butler, R. N. (1974). Life review therapy. *Geriatrics, 29*(11), 165–173.

Lidoff, L. (1984). Sharing a common concern. *Perspective on Aging, 13*(1), 26–27.

Lindemann, E. (1944). Symptomatology and management of acute grief. *American Journal of Psychiatry, 101*(2), 141–148.

Loewenstein, S. (1977). An overview of the concept of narcissism. *Social Casework, 59*(2), 106–115.

Loewenstein, S. (1978). An overview of some aspects of female sexuality. *Social Casework, 59*(2), 106–115.

Lukton, R. C. (1982). Myths and realities of crisis intervention. *Social Casework, 63*(5), 276–285.

Lyon, E., Silverman, M. L., Howe, G. W., Bishop, G., & Armstrong, B. (1985). Stages of divorce: Implications for service delivery. *Social Casework, 66*(5), 259–267.

McMahon, A, & Rhudick, P. (1964). Reminiscing: Adaptational significance in the aged. *Archives of General Psychiatry, 10*(3), 292–298.

Maddison, D., Viola, A., & Walker, W. (1969). Further studies in conjugal bereavement. *Australian and New Zealand Journal of Psychiatry, 3*(63).

Marris, P. (1975). *Loss and change.* Garden City, NY: Anchor Press.

Martini Beaulieu, E. & Karpinski, J. (1981). Group treatment of elderly with ill spouses. *Social Casework, 62*(9), 551–557.

Masters, W. H., & Johnson, V. E. (1966). *Human sexual response.* Boston: Little, Brown & Co.

Mead, M. (1972). *Blackberry winter.* New York: William Morrow & Co.

Meerloo, J. (1961). Modes of psychotherapy in the aged. *Journal of the American Geriatrics Society, 9*(3), 225–234.

Melito, R. (1985). Adaptation in family systems: A developmental perspective. *Family Process, 24*(1), 89–100.

Monson, R. G. (1981, July/August). The greying of the American Jewish community: Implications of changing family patterns for communal institutions. *Conservative Judaism,* 52–56.

Neugarten, B. L. (1964). *Personality in middle and late life.* New York: Atherton Press.

Neugarten, B. L. (1970). Dynamics of transition of middle-age to old age. *Journal of Geriatric Psychiatry, 4*(1), 71–87.

Neugarten, B. L. & Datan, N. (1973). Sociological perspectives with life cycle. In P. B. Baltes & K. W. Shaie (Eds.), *Life-span developmental psychology: Personality and socialization* (pp. 53–71). New York: Academic Press.

Offer, D., & Sabshin, M. (Eds.). (1984). *Normality and the life cycle: A critical integration.* New York: Basic Books.

Pedrick-Cornell, C., & Gelles, R. J., (1982). Elder abuse: The status of current knowledge. *Family Relations, 31*(3), 457–465.

Pratt, C. C., Koval, J. & Lloyd, S. (1983). Service workers' responses to abuse of the elderly. *Social Casework, 64*(3), 147–153.

Psychology Today (1985, March). *Crosstalk, 19*(3), p. 8.

Rathbone-McCuen, E. (1980). Elderly victims of family violence and neglect. *Social Casework, 61*(5), 296–304.

Rathbone-McCuen, E., & Bland, J. (1975). A treatment typology for the elderly alcohol abuser. *Journal of the American Geriatric Society, 23*(12), 553–557.

Rathbone-McCuen, E., & Voles, B. (1982). Case detection of abused elderly parents. *American Journal of Psychiatry 139*(2), 189–192.

Reid, M. T. (1985). My use of photographs in therapy. *Phototherapy, IV*(3), 10–12.

Reid, W. J., & Epstein, L. (1972). *Task-centered casework.* New York: Columbia University Press.

Rhodes, S. L. (1977). A developmental approach to the life cycle in the family. *Social Casework, 58*(5), 301–311.

Rivinus, T. M., & Gutheil, T. G. (1977). When the insurance money runs out. *Psychiatric Annals, 7*(2), 96–111.

Romaniuk, M. Reminiscence and the second half of life: A review. Unpublished paper in Getzel, G. (1983). Intergenerational reminiscence in groups of the frail elderly. *The Journal of Jewish Communal Service 59*(4), 515–521.

Rosenberg, E. B., & Hajal, F. (1985). Stepsibling relationships in remarried families. *Social Casework, 66*(5), 287–292.

Rubin, R. (1977). Learning to overcome reluctance for psychotherapy with the elderly. *Journal of Geriatric Psychiatry, 10*(2), 215–227.

Sander, F. (1976). Aspects of sexual counseling with the aged. *Social Casework, 57*(8), 504–510.

Saferstein, S. L. (1967). Institutional transference. *Psychiatric Quarterly, 41*(3), 557–566.

Sargent, S. S. (Ed.) (1980). *Nontraditional therapy and counseling with the aged.* New York: Springer.

Satir, V. M. (1964). *Conjoint family therapy.* Palo Alto, CA: Science and Behavior Books.

Savitsky, E., & Sharkey, H. (1973). The geriatric patient and his family:

Study of the family interaction in the aged. *Journal of Geriatric Psychiatry, 5*(1), 3–24.

Seskin, J. (1985). *Alone but not lonely: Independent living for women over fifty.* Scott, Foresman & Co., Illinois: Lifelong Learning Division.

Shain, D. D. (1977). Group counseling with Jewish elderly. *Journal of Jewish Communal Service, 53*(4), 383–388.

Sheehy, G. (1976). *Passages.* New York: E. P. Dutton.

Shulman, S. C. (1985). Psychodynamic group therapy with older women. *Social Casework, 66*(10), 579–586.

Silverman, A. G., Kahn, B. M., & Anderson, G. (1977). A model for working with multigenerational families. *Social Casework, 58*(3), 131–135.

Simon, D. S. (1976). A systematic approach to family life education. *Social Casework, 57*(8), 511–516.

Solomon, M. A. (1973). A developmental conceptual premise for family therapy. *Family Process, 12*(2), 179–188.

Solomon, M. A. (1977). The staging of family treatment: An approach to developing the therapeutic alliance. *Journal of Marriage and Family Counseling, 3*(2), 59–66.

Spakes, P. R. (1979). Family, friendships and community interaction as related to life satisfaction of the elderly. *Journal of Gerontological Social Work, 1*(4), 279–293.

Speck, R. V., & Atteneave, C. L. (1973). *Family networks.* New York: Pantheon Books.

Stambler, M. (1982). Jewish ethnicity and aging. *Journal of Jewish Communal Service, 58*(4), 336–342.

Stein, H. D., & Cloward, R. A. (Eds.) (1958). *Social perspectives on behavior.* Glencoe, IL: Free Press.

Sze, W. C. (1975). *Human life cycle.* New York: Jason Aronson.

Thomas, L. (1981, April). On the problem of dementia. *Discover,* pp. 34–36.

Toseland, R. W., & Hacker, L. (1982). Self-help groups and professional involvement. *Social Work, 27*(4), 341–347.

Turner, H. (Ed.). (1967). *Psychological function of older people.* New York: National Council on Aging.

Twente, E. E. (1970). *Never too old.* San Francisco: Jossey-Bass.

Vaillant, G. E. (1977). *Adaptation to Life.* Boston: Little, Brown.

Verwoerdt, E. (1976). *Clinical geropsychiatry.* Baltimore MD: Williams & Wilkins.

Visher, E. B., & Visher, J. S. (1979). *Stepfamilies: A guide to working with stepparents and stepchildren.* New York: Brunner/Mazel.

von Oech, R. (1983). *A whack on the side of the head.* New York: Warner Books.

Wasow, M. (1986). Support groups for family caregivers of patients with Alzheimer's disease. *Social Work, 31*(2), 93–97.

Wasser, E. (1966). *Creative approaches in casework with the aging.* New York: Family Service Association of America.

Weakland, J., Fisch, R., Watzlawick, P., & Bodin, A. M. (1974). Brief therapy: focused problem resolution. *Family Process, 13*(2), 141–168.

Weick, A. (1983). A growth-task model of human development. *Social Casework, 64*(3), 131–137.

Weiner, M. Ruth Hutton Fred Lecture, Baylor University College of Medicine, March 20, 1985, Houston, Texas. Group treatment with the aged. Unpublished paper.

Wells, C. E. (1979). Pseudodementia. *American Journal of Psychiatry, 136*(7), 859–900.

Werman, D. S. (1984). *The practice of supportive psychotherapy.* New York: Brunner/Mazel.

Werner, J. N., & Varner, R. V. (1983). Marital crisis in late life: Too late for therapy? *The Journal, Houston International Hospital 2*(2), 17–20.

Whitaker, C. A. (1981). The normal family. Unpublished paper presented at the National Family Therapy Institute, San Antonio, Texas.

Williams, M., Roback, H. B., & Pro, J. (1980). A geriatric growth group. *Group, 4*(3), 43–48.

Wolinsky, M. A. (1985). Consultation: A treatment model for the aging and their families. *Social Casework, 66*(11), 540–546.

Wolinsky, M. A. (1986). Marital therapy with older couples. *Social Casework, 67*(10), 475–483.

Workshop Proceedings of University of Texas Medical Branch, Enhancing Health and Life Styles. Galveston, Texas, September, 1978.

Zacks, H. (1980). Self-actualization: A mid-life problem. *Social Casework, 61*(4), 223–233.

Zentner, E. B., & Zentner, M. (1985). The psychomechanic nonchemical management of depression. *Social Casework, 66*(5), 275–286.

Subject Index

Name Index

Ackerman, N. W., 15
Altholz, J., 160, 162
American Association of Retired
    Persons and Administration on
    Aging, 2, 30
Arendt, H., 40

Barrow, G. M., 8, 9
Blau, Z., 15
Blazer, D., 49, 54, 123, 175, 193
Blenkner, M., 12, 37
Bloch, D., 84
Bockus, F., 110
Boszormenyi-Nagy, I., 11, 12, 142
Bowen, M., 110
Bowlby, J., 56, 122, 123, 130, 131
Brennan, E., 36
Brink, T. L., 172, 175, 177, 178
Brody, E. M., 156
Busse, E. W., 155, 165
Butler, R., x, 55, 106–108, 112

Carter, E. A., 16, 19, 23, 73, 94, 96–
    105
Cath, S., 56
Christ, J., 16, 126, 130–132
Cloward, R. A., 15
Cohen, R. G., 187

Datan, N., 9, 94
Duhl, J., 164

Engel, G., 131
Epstein, L., 148

Erikson, E., 51, 81, 87, 90, 106, 107

Feldman, L. B., 75
Fenichel, O., 45
Fontane, A. S., 74
Framo, J. L., 64
Freud, S., 6, 123, 131, 175

Getzel, G. S., 29, 107, 111, 162
Glick, I. D., 23, 73
Goldfarb, A. I., 3, 161, 175
Greene, B. L., 65, 66, 84
Greene, R. R., 171, 180
Grunebaum, H., 16, 126, 130–132

Haley, J., 65, 91
Hellebrandt, F. A., 2

Johnson, V. E., 43
Jung, C. G., 170

Kastenbaum, R., 174, 179
Kernberg, O., 45
Kessler, D. R., 23, 73
Kubler-Ross, E., 134

Lebowitz, B. D., 31, 184
Levinson, D. J., 88, 107
Lidoff, L., 163
Loewenstein, S., 45

Maddison, D., 132
Masters, W. H., 43
McGoldrick, M., 16, 19, 23, 73, 94,
    96–105